Learning
from
business
leaders

Learning from business leaders

A Coaching Memoir

Dr. Monica McGrath

Published by Grammar Factory Publishing, an imprint of MacMillan
Company Limited.

Grammar Factory Publishing
MacMillan Company Limited
25 Telegram Mews, 39th Floor, Suite 3906
Toronto, Ontario, Canada
M5V 3Z1

www.grammarfactory.com

McGrath, Dr. Monica.
Learning From Business Leaders: A Coaching Memoir / Dr. Monica
McGrath.

Paperback ISBN 978-1-998756-67-4
Hardcover ISBN 978-1-998756-69-8
eBook ISBN 978-1-998756-68-1

1. BUS071000 BUSINESS & ECONOMICS / Leadership. 2. BUS103000
BUSINESS & ECONOMICS / Organizational Development.
3. BUS106000 BUSINESS & ECONOMICS / Mentoring & Coaching.

Production Credits
Cover design by Designerbility
Interior layout design by Setareh Ashrafologhalai
Book production and editorial services by Grammar Factory Publishing

Grammar Factory's Carbon Neutral Publishing Commitment
Grammar Factory Publishing is proud to be neutralizing the carbon
footprint of all printed copies of its authors' books printed by or ordered
directly through Grammar Factory or its affiliated companies through the
purchase of Gold Standard-Certified International Offsets.

DISCLAIMER

I have recreated the events and conversations detailed in this book to the best of my ability, based on my memories. In order to maintain anonymity, I have changed the names of individuals, places, and companies. I have also changed some identifying characteristics and details, such as physical properties, job titles, and places of residence.

CONTENTS

ACKNOWLEDGMENTS

AM GRATEFUL FOR the opportunity to be a part of the working life of my clients, colleagues, and students. Their openness as they faced challenges served as my classroom and this book is a thank-you letter to all of you.

To my family—Jim, Karin, Mike, Charlotte and Julian, Patrick, Lilliana, and Santiago. You reflect the best of me, and this book is yours as well as mine.

To my writing coaches and supporters: Kathy Morris, Kevin Garcia, Nancy Rasmussen, Rosemary LeCompte, Dan McElhatton, Diane Davis, and Kathleen Burns—thank you for your encouragement, feedback, and optimism. This work is a result of the positivity you bring to my life.

INTRODUCTION
COURAGEOUS
MEN AND WOMEN

N A SHORT conversation with a colleague, a top executive managing a billion-dollar budget, we spent our time trying to figure out how to change the behavior of one of her most important staff members—her staff manager. This executive was frustrated, annoyed, and confused with her manager. This employee was creative and smart, so how, my client wondered, could she be so blind to the impact of her short-tempered responses to legitimate concerns, and why would she discount and dismiss others' ideas? This behavior was arrogant. It seemed obvious to some and had a serious impact on others. My client thought her staff manager was building resentment and anger among her team members, almost assuring collaboration on important initiatives was impossible.

Shortly after this conversation, I took a call from a former student. He called to see if I had any ideas about how to deal with the corporate "suits" he was now working with. They were so slow to make decisions that he felt they were deliberately stifling progress on strategic goals. He was ready to quit.

In both situations, these people felt trapped. Despite being experienced, well-educated and successful people in their respective fields, they felt exhausted by problems that might, and often did, derail their well-intentioned efforts to advance their enterprises. They had become immobilized and were not able to cope with the day-to-day stressors embedded in a leader's role. Yes, they could walk away from these jobs and find others. Certainly, there is evidence that in these post-pandemic times, some of the most ambitious and competent leaders publicly walk away from the stress of caring for their people. Of course, this isn't a new trend. Walking away from stressful roles and "quiet quitting" happened before the global scourge of the pandemic. The day-to-day challenges, frustrations, and skepticism inherent in a leader's role can slowly erode the confidence and enthusiasm of anyone.

Does this sound familiar? Is it you? Or is it one of your team members, perhaps? Will you act, or will you wonder what happened to the person you hired who had such enthusiasm and optimism? Will you turn to your coach, if you have one, or to your own insights and reflections to address these day-to-day issues? Will you use the resources of management professionals, coupled with your own experiences and self-knowledge, to deepen your understanding of the realities of leading? Will you support those who are open and willing to raise their hand when they are asked to lead?

If you are willing to learn, then this book is for you. It is for the courageous men and women who make the decision to take on a leadership role and for those who serve them as coaches, mentors, and friends. I will tell a series of stories that you may find familiar— the political intrigue, the team that works, the board that doesn't. But what's different about this leadership book is the perspective given by the outsider, an experienced executive coach. The business coach has a trusted seat next to the leader. Coaches work with all types of business men and women, but the stories in this book highlight the leader who is curious and open to learning. The stories and the learning that happened because of a coach's reflections go beyond inspirational quotes and tap into the insights, tools, and tips from the experience of experts committed to developing strong and focused leaders. So, with that in mind, allow me to introduce myself.

A front-row seat to leadership challenges

My name is Doctor Monica McGrath. I have over thirty years of experience working with leaders. I've worked in all manner of roles, including as a salesperson, a trainer, a consultant, an adjunct professor, a vice dean, and an executive coach. I've worked in my own consulting company, collaborating with leaders at every level in their quest to learn and grow, and I've worked inside organizations and educational institutions, leading teams and being accountable for results.

From the first time I realized that the business world was rich with intrigue—and full of human stories of courage, failure, achievement, and adventure—I was smitten. From my first leadership role, as the president of my Junior Achievement class in 1963, through to today, when I am still coaching and counseling leaders at every level, I have sought the experience and education to be able to weave psychology, business, and teaching into my career tapestry.

My educational background includes a degree in psychology and a PhD in adult learning and organizational dynamics. In every job, every coaching assignment, and every consulting gig, I've had a front-row seat to the challenges business leaders face. My higher education, which was delayed twenty years after high school, taught me how to ask the right kinds of questions of those who shared their business dilemmas with me. My knowledge of organizational psychology, my background in educational theory, and my curiosity about how leaders develop themselves allowed me to create a safe and supportive forum for business leaders to explore their actions and understand their motivations, emotions, and values, with a goal to enhance their approach to leadership.

Why I wrote this book— and what you'll learn

Initially, I wrote this book for my children, grand-children, and dear nieces and nephews. When they talk about their jobs, I have often wished that I could share a story or lesson from my career that might help them (though I realize it's not always easy to receive unsolicited advice). However, as I wrote about the experiences of my career, I realized that I actually wrote this book for me.

I don't anticipate that this book will become a bestseller, and I don't think of myself as a coaching guru. Rather, I thought I might be able to use the book during my workshops and seminars, and I intend to do so. I also found myself uninterested in writing anything overly academic or instructional, mainly because I felt depleted after writing my dissertation. Now, as my career is in a phase of creative reinvention, I find myself with vivid memories of those clients, students, and colleagues who invited me into their world and became my learning partners. I wrote this book to capture the lessons of my life and to reinforce my hope that I am not yet finished on the path of learning.

This book is for anyone who chooses to take on a leadership role or who may wish to support some-one in this position. It captures the important and essential lessons from the day-to-day challenges and rewards of those in leadership.

What are the key takeaways? Through a series of real-life stories, I will:

- Provide insight into the real work of those in leadership roles.

- Explore the research around leadership, and share tips and tools to enhance your leadership.

- Share how I, as an experienced executive coach, use personal insight, reflection, and observation skills to enhance my practice.

If you are tired of leadership being simplified into cliched phrases, memes, and lovely but overused quotes, I encourage you to read on. This book will introduce you to real leadership challenges as well as the deep questions they pose and the resources that can help drive a leader's success.

1

THE ROCK STAR
IN JAPAN

S I WALKED down the hallway toward the boardroom of this global auto company, I felt a sense
of accomplishment and a flutter of excitement.
This meeting and my pitch to a well-known Japanese
automaker might result in a long-term relationship
with the company and with an iconic CEO. The goal
today was to gain the approval of the CEO on the
delivery of an executive leadership program. I hoped
to be the faculty director of this program; teaching the
leaders of the largest automobile group in the world
would advance my skills and my reputation.

I was here in Japan along with three professors:
one from our business school (one of the top schools
in the world) and two from a prestigious university in
Japan. In my role leading executive programs for the
school, I had been working to arrange this meeting
for months. And I was nervous about the meeting.
The full tour was impressive. It reminded us that this

was a Japanese company with pride in its past and a determination to own the future. The headquarters was a sprawling, glass-encased, modern building. Sparkling model cars of all kinds were showcased on the entry floor, highlighting the impressive history of the company, as well as futuristic models of cars our grandchildren might be driving someday. I grew increasingly nervous, knowing I would soon be meeting with a business school icon—the CEO.

My MBA students always found our discussions and case studies on this CEO inspiring. He had made substantive changes in the company when he came to Japan, and he had built a culture of accountability and results. They found his leadership inspiring and courageous, and their respect for him was palpable. He was, in their estimation and mine, a rock star. The class discussions about this company and this leader were always lively and provocative. How he, an outsider, managed to rebuild the company in 1999 made him a legend. I hoped that my face-to-face meeting with him and his possible engagement in this leadership class we were hoping to deliver would add even more color to my MBA classroom discussions.

But I was stopped in my tracks as I walked toward the boardroom. The human resource manager turned to me and said, "*Don't ask him about his wife.*" I was stunned. I looked over at my male colleagues as they calmly chatted with one another, and I realized this comment was directed solely at me, the only woman in the entourage. Wow. Could this manager think I cared more about the CEO's spousal situation than my role as the head of the business school's executive learning division? And, despite my knowledge that Japan is decades behind other nations in terms of women's rights, could this manager think so little of my competence that he thought I would forget what I was there to do? I was suddenly angry and distracted just minutes before the meeting. I reacted to him with icy silence.

We proceeded into the boardroom, and I decided to assert my presence immediately as I positioned myself facing the CEO. The only other women in the room were serving tea and taking notes. While I tried to remain inclusive and kind, I was upset and disoriented. I was also determined to prove my competence and get things back on track. When we began our pitch for the leadership program, one that this CEO hoped would solidify his legacy, I realized that we had already won this job, thanks to the reputation of our school and the credibility of the Japanese faculty members who knew the company. As the meeting ended with a cordial goodbye, the CEO expressed that he would like to be a part of the program as a faculty member, and we agreed with enthusiasm.

My nervousness abated as I walked away, and within a few hours, I stopped thinking about the comment that had triggered my anger. But later, I realized something had changed in me during that meeting. Even after decades of experience, a prestigious role, and a well-earned doctorate, I was still facing the antiquated view that women were not really business-oriented. On my flight back to Philadelphia, I wondered if all my efforts to help change that view were for nothing. I wondered if my frustration and anger were about the slow pace of change regarding the perception of female leaders or if I simply overreacted due to my anxiety about the meeting.

KEY QUESTIONS

Even though this global leader would be arrested for fraud and be the subject of scandal within the next few years, I was still feeling anger years later when I took the time to examine the learning moments from that momentous trip. Looking for insight and lessons within a challenge is one of the best ways to enhance your leadership learning. When I reflected on the meeting in Japan later—after the dramatic ending to the CEO's career—I asked myself the following questions:

- What was my role in that exchange?

- Did I check my expectations and my emotions before I walked into the boardroom?

- How had the comment before the meeting influenced my behavior in the meeting?

- Should I have said something about the inappropriate comment?

- Was the icy silence a cop-out or an appropriate response, given the situation?

Questions like these, as you will note throughout this book, lead me to research, to further my education as a business-oriented psychologist, and to continually broaden and inform my life experiences.

Leadership Lessons

The ability to capture leadership lessons embedded in both positive and negative work challenges is the essence of leader development. Here are six leadership lessons I took away from the experience in Japan.

Assess your emotional intelligence

Emotional intelligence is not just the latest business fad. It is a set of skills that every business leader must master. While the term "emotional intelligence" has been in the business lexicon for many decades, I often find executives misunderstand the term and, frankly, get confused about what it all means and why it matters. A simple definition, adapted from ability-based scholars, is this: emotional intelligence helps you to know your own emotions, to read and decipher the emotions of others, and to manage your emotions in service to your values and goals.

So, how might you assess and enhance your emotional intelligence or EI? The popularity of the concept has spawned numerous tests for EI, but I believe the best resources for learning more about EI can be found at the EI Consortium (eiconsortium.org).

Learn to use the language of emotions

Some managers and executives think feelings have little to do with business. They are wrong—very wrong. Think about it. Do you have a story about how you were the recipient of an angry exchange for which a boss later apologized? Did you ever see a nervous and excited presenter lose a sale because she was so concerned about her own anxiety that she forgot to listen? It helps to know the language of emotions and moods. Are you tired? Does your boss seem irritated? Is your teammate depressed? If you enhance your ability to identify emotions, you will be better at deciphering what you see in others and factoring in how those emotions will help or hinder your goals. Again, the popularity of the concept of EI has spawned numerous online resources and assessments to determine your level of skill, but many of these tests are overwhelming in their definition of EI. Think of EI as a competency, an ability, and one you can learn. A quick scan of the EI Consortium website (eiconsortium.org) will give you a plan for learning how to talk about emotions, and how to manage and use them as well.

Prepare for the room

Prepare for the emotions in the room well before your meeting. In Japan, I had prepared the pricing, the course work, the timing, and the powerful role of the CEO and his team, but I did not factor in how I was feeling. I certainly could have considered what the human resource team might have been feeling. How about the faculty team? While your predictions of others' emotions may not always be accurate, you will be better prepared for unanticipated distractions if you consider the emotional energy and moods that might be present in the meeting room. The impact of your own emotions will need your attention, too. Taking time to consider and acknowledge your emotional state will help you to better manage your responses. Without awareness of how a room and the people in it feel, you risk reactions that might drive your idea to dust.

Analyze the group

When you are presenting to others, and particularly when you are hoping to influence others, do you consider their stake in your goal? While it is tricky to make assumptions about how they might react, behave, or respond to your ideas, it is often useful to use your analytical skills to anticipate how others may react. This is easy when you have previously worked with a group, but less so if you do not really know them. But it can be done.

Take the time to write down what you know about each person in the group. If you get stuck, try to put yourself in their position. Ask yourself what they could gain by adopting your ideas. What might they lose? What might you say or do if you were sitting in their seat at the table? Once you do this, prepare a response that you can practice, and you will be so much better prepared. While it does take time to do this type of preparation, ask yourself if this analysis of others' reactions is less important than the time spent preparing for the financial impact of your idea.

Manage your own reactions

Before my meeting with the company in Japan, I planned how I would talk about the school, the reputation of the faculty members who would teach in the program, the pricing, and the participant demographics. I did not plan for how the team from the company might react to this meeting with the CEO. I never considered how the faculty would participate or what they wanted from this interaction with the CEO. If I had been less starstruck, I might have noticed my stress level and nervous energy and managed myself from the first hour we toured the building. If I had been more attentive to my peers, the managers, and the women who were taking notes, I would have added positive energy to the meeting and walked away from it feeling less anger and more confidence.

Here is how my analysis might have gone:

The HR manager: I hosted the HR manager in Philadelphia when he toured our facilities. We had spent informal time together, and I knew he was curious about me and my role as a vice dean. He knew I was an ardent advocate for women's educational opportunities. In our time together, we discussed a recently released study, which had ranked Japan 104th among 136 countries with women in executive roles. He also knew I had hoped to bring Japanese women from his company to our university MBA program. Given this, is it possible that he was reacting to his own fears and was concerned that I would advocate a feminist agenda in front of the CEO? Was he worried that I would embarrass him and bring up the dismal results of the report we had discussed? I eventually came to think that his remark was not intended as a personal affront but was perhaps a projection of his anxiety.

The professors: I was traveling with a professor who was known for his arrogance, but he was an intellectual with a vast knowledge of the history of Japan and Asia more broadly. He was also known for his abysmal track record in the classroom and his alienation of female faculty members. I knew all this and intuitively knew that he would not want to highlight the content of the coursework. Instead, it was probable that he would try to distract others with stories of his travels in Asia, and he would be driven to impress the CEO and the Japanese faculty members. Once we were assembled, if I had prepared appropriately, I would have managed the agenda and called on the professors when needed. My physical position in the middle of the table was strategic and a good idea. However, I could have taken time to role-play the agenda with the faculty members. Perhaps this would have allowed me to confidently share my expertise in course design and leader development.

Debrief and learn
You may be thinking that you don't have the time to do a rigorous review of every important meeting. Yet

there is evidence that you learn the most from your most challenging leadership moments. Having the discipline to conduct an after-action review on your own unique experience will ensure you capture every lesson you need to advance and enhance your leadership. To quote Nike, "Just Do It." In this case, the course did proceed; the school delivered the program five times, and I attended the first offering—although we never saw the CEO, even before his messy career demise. Still, I thank him and the company for the opportunity to learn more than I had ever imagined that afternoon in Yokohama.

References

Bekhouche, Y., Hausmann, R., Tyson, L. D., & Zahidi, S. (2014, October 20). The global gender gap report 2014. World Economic Forum. https://www.weforum.org/reports/global-gender-gap-report-2014/

Consortium for Research on Emotional Intelligence in Organizations. https://www.eiconsortium.org

Leggett, T. (2021, August 3). The downfall of Nissan's Carlos Ghosn: An insider's view. BBC News. https://www.bbc.com/news/business-58070929

2

A STEADY COMPASS
AMID TRAGEDY

"A GREAT GUY" was how Bob, my new client, was described to me. I took off in my car to meet him on a crisp and clear day in September. It was an hour's drive north from my home, so I put on some calming music and began to think through my coaching approach. I thought about what I knew so far and wondered what this great guy—a designated "high potential" leader—might learn from an executive coach.

I enjoyed my work with this Fortune 500 consumer brand company. Established in the 1800s and with a global workforce of almost 35,000 people, you would probably recognize the brand no matter where in the world you were. Bob was the director of research for the company's oral care division, and toothpaste was this company's lifeline. Bob had received excellent ratings on a recent 360-degree survey, but the human resource division thought he might be thinking about leaving the company if he was not promoted soon. While deserved, his advancement might take a few years because his boss was not thinking of retiring any time soon. Bob seemed to be the perfect fit for the future—a skilled dentist in private practice who was recruited with the lure of a substantial bonus, the promise of advancement, and stock options. Human resource professionals shared this information with me, and while I felt very prepared for this assignment, I would learn a lot more about Bob in this upcoming meeting. It would be brief but revealing.

I had arrived a few minutes before the 9 a.m. scheduled meeting and found the reception area unusually empty. I had been here many times before and was always warmly greeted by the reception-ist, who would offer coffee, call my client, and chat briefly while I waited to be shown to an office. But not today. Today, the receptionist was with her colleagues, watching in shock as footage played on the TV of the first plane hitting the North Tower of the World Trade Center. After the second tower was hit, Bob came to find me and told me what was happening. We slowly walked together toward the group assembled in front of the television and watched in horror as 9/11 con-tinued to unfold. Bob finally turned to me and, with tears in his eyes, apologized for canceling our time together. He said he really needed to find out how his team was taking this news and how this would affect the corporate office in Midtown Manhattan. He even had the calm foresight to ask me if I knew anyone who worked in the towers and whether I would be okay driving back to my office. He knew he could not really concentrate, and I wholeheartedly agreed.

KEY QUESTIONS

These questions, and others, are the ones many of us were struggling with on that morning:

- What did I learn that morning about myself?

- What did I learn about Bob?

- What was the role of values in this scenario?

- What does a leader do under circumstances like these?

- What is the approach one should take when disrupted by unforeseen events or conditions?

Leadership Lessons

Watching Bob respond in that moment provided many lessons for me. Here are four leadership lessons I took away from the experience.

Know what matters most

Bob and I worked together for over six months and met or talked frequently over a few years when we connected through social media. On that fateful day Bob's actions were informed by his values—a calming presence, patience and concern, easily accessed empathy and kindness—but these were always a part of his style. His behavior never faltered in the months we worked together and as we planned his strategy for the future.

The actions you take are informed by values, and these values are the fundamental platform for a leader's behavior, even in a crisis as dramatic as 9/11 or the COVID-19 pandemic. But we don't often think about our values. Bob was no exception, but he did know what really mattered to him as a result of tragic life circumstances. As I learned more about him and his story, it was evident that he had been prepared by events in his own life for that tragic morning in September 2001.

Bob had been widowed in his early years when his young wife died from cancer. Bob cared for her during her illness even as he continued his career and education. And even now, a decade later, as he told me his story, his grief was palpable. Bob had eventually remarried and had a growing family with two small children. His own sad history taught him that even in the prime of life, there are setbacks that can crush you. Supportive, empathetic, and kind friends were Bob's bulwark, and he never forgot the lessons he learned from his difficult time of life. He nurtured those lessons in his personal life and, really, in all areas of his life—work included. We all have values at the center of our lives, and as we take on leadership roles, we need to remember what matters to us.

There is an assessment called the Rokeach Value Survey. I learned about this early in my career and scholarly work on values. The survey is easy to take and still applicable today. In fact, all rising executives should use some version of this tool often throughout their careers. The Rokeach Value Survey defines core values in two distinct categories: instrumental values and terminal values. Terminal values define an end state—the goal you strive to reach. Instrumental values are the path you want to follow to achieve that goal. For example, I prioritize as one of my top five terminal values "an exciting life," and the instrumental value I want and need to achieve that is "courageousness." Of course, you are not defined solely by one value, but you are not defined by twenty, either. And values will change over your lifetime based on your personal and professional realities.

Here is another example of how this works: there was a time in my life when an exciting life meant a hiking trip to the Himalayas, and I needed courage to make that trip. Later in my life, an exciting life meant I would take on a new and demanding job. Knowing what matters to me when faced with a decision can help me overcome any hesitation. When invited to take on a new challenge, my decision often supports my value of an exciting life. Similarly, Bob was clear about his values. One of his top priorities was family security, which was defined in the survey as "taking care of loved ones." It's no surprise, then, that his behavior on the heartbreaking morning of September 11th was helpful, responsible, and empathetic.

Develop the habit

It is impossible to know when you will be asked to lead during a crisis. We have all seen the scourge of the pandemic, as well as unforeseen tragedy and grief in our workplaces and homes. On 9/11, Bob did not hesitate when he was needed as the leader of his team. He did not have to think about how to act since he had developed the habit of connecting to others with kindness even when hit with such an unexpected tragedy. When we are asked to step up to leadership, the prepared and focused leader will draw on past experiences and the leadership habits that make the challenging steps easier to climb.

Award-winning Wharton Professor Katy Milkman published a book titled *How to Change*, reiterating the science of behavior change. She recommends these simple tips to help you build the habits of behavior that will always reflect your best self:

1. Allow yourself to be flexible and forgive your mistakes.

2. Be certain to reward your good efforts.

Bob's case is a good example of how he built the habits that were second nature to him on that fateful day we first met. While Bob had a supportive family and a deep faith to lean on after the death of his wife, it would have been understandable for him to succumb to guilt or regret. But he made another choice—he chose to live life fully and in service to others with a penchant for forgiveness. He vowed to do the best he could for others because of his own loss and forgive himself for any shortcomings while consciously making it a habit to forgive others for theirs.

Bob found personal satisfaction in the success of his team. He derived pleasure from advancing one of his employees, and he had a habit of serving others. He expressed happiness for their accomplishments, publicly and privately. In many ways, Bob demonstrated how his intention to serve others matched his actions by always being positive and supportive when someone achieved success. He had the habit of showing his team how much he cared for them and was even able to do this on a day when fear, anger, and confusion reigned.

Love your people

Bob had a good reputation. He acknowledged the contribution of his team, and he gave them access to important meetings, conferences, and projects. Bob sincerely wanted others to do well, he was humble, and he loved his team. Are you surprised to read the word "love" in the last sentence? Scholars like Professor Sigal Barsade, who study organizational culture, have observed that feelings of tenderness, affection, and care improve employee outcomes. This is known as companionate love. A work culture of the type Bob created, which was rich with empathy and caring, is known to have a positive impact on an employee's mood and improve work satisfaction.

I think we have become more comfortable with the idea that we often love those with whom we work. It is rare for someone who leads loyal, competent, and hardworking team members not to feel love for them. You can learn to demonstrate companionate love by expressing appreciation, listening to the dreams and ambitions of your employees, and making sure to highlight the accomplishments of your team. Bob was a shining example of someone who loved his team, and he was someone everyone wanted to work for.

Love yourself

The only negative feedback Bob ever received was that he was too humble, too nice, and not aggressive enough. This type of feedback is paradoxical and confusing. One possible response to that type of feedback is to try to make a significant change in your behavior. But no one is fooled, and these efforts are often met with cynicism or seen as comical. Another response could be to blame the company and the culture for the aggressive and competitive behavior that is often rewarded in the C-suite. Either response is likely to stall or derail an otherwise competent leader. Humility can be misread as low self-esteem or a weakness, but humble leaders are confident enough that they often don't see the need to broadcast their competence. The research is fairly evident that someone defined as a humble leader benefits from less turnover in the employee ranks and is more likely to cultivate continual improvement in employee productivity and communication.

In Bob's case, his humble approach was perceived as weak and resulted in the assumption by some that he was not able to win the attention of the top team when he needed to influence critical initiatives. This perception stalled Bob's advancement and was the reason he thought he would need to leave the company if he was to advance. I worked with Bob to help him address his frustration with the company and to help him craft strategies for advancement. While he continued to bring a humble and kind presence to his work, he also started to point out to the top team the exceptional results he and his team delivered, and he spoke more freely about the strategic decisions he made in his leadership role. These efforts influenced the decision-makers and their opinion about Bob's future at the company.

Bob did eventually advance, becoming a senior vice president. He continued to be a beloved leader while also driving initiatives and results. When he retired early from the company, he was lauded for his humility and kindness. And it was no surprise to anyone that after retirement, he began a new career as a religious leader and spiritual counselor in his church community.

References

Barsade, S., & O'Neill, O. (2014, May 29). What's love got to do with it? A longitudinal study of the culture of companionate love and employee and client outcomes in a long-term care setting. Sage Journals. https://journals.sagepub.com/doi/10.1177/0001839214538636

Hanel, P. H. P., Litzellachner, L. F., & Maio, G. R. (2018, August 16). An empirical comparison of human value models. Frontiers. https://www.frontiersin.org/articles/10.3389/fpsyg.2018.01643/full

Rokeach, M. (1977). The nature of human values. Free Press.

3

A LEAGUE OF
HIS OWN

IMMEDIATELY NOTICED THE baseball bat in the
corner of Ron's office that first day. I love baseball
and, in my naiveté, thought the bat belonged to
Ron's son, left there after a recent practice. I had been
sent by my employer to finalize a coaching contract
for Ron, who had just received a promotion and a
plum assignment heading three of the company's
major manufacturing plants. Later, I learned that the
bat was one of the reasons I was sitting in this impos-
ing office of a top executive.

Ron worked in an industry that had been the back-
bone of the US economy since the nineteenth century.
Ron's company was once the largest employer in
America. But on that day in the mid-1990s, the company and the industry more broadly were struggling
to survive. So, to revitalize the company, the top brass
began targeted efforts to upgrade the skills of their
employees, and Ron was at the center of that target.

Ron was a financial wizard with an almost religious commitment to the quality standards of the company's products and the safety of its employees. This combination was just what the top brass needed, and thus, Ron became a candidate for coaching.

The consulting company I was working for was reluctant to take on this company as a client. The suits, as we called the leadership team, had little interest in working in a small-town manufacturing facility with those whom they imagined wore hard hats, yellow vests, and steel-toed boots. With my newly minted PhD and a sense of adventure, I thought the hard hats and gritty plant floor sounded just fine. As soon as I was asked to head to the Midwest to meet this new client, I booked the flight, rented the car, and was on my way.

I had been informed that Ron knew he was poised for advancement in the company. He was a very good accountant, and his expertise helped him focus on the numbers, but he also seemed to be aware of his limitations. The human side of the business was not his strong suit. His new assignment would mean he would lead hundreds of employees, and his teams were in three different cities. Yes, he had some work to do. He needed some help as he attempted to lead more effectively and send the signal to upper management that he was more than a numbers guy.

That first meeting was tense and unsettling. Ron was skeptical. He immediately mentioned that he did not like consultants. I suspected that, given the paucity of women in the company, the fact that I was female and a consultant was a double whammy. While Ron was cautious and guarded, I felt as if I was on trial. As we began our conversation, Ron asked me about my background, my education, and how I came to be sitting in his office. I was honest about my undergraduate education, which began in my late thirties, and my month-old doctorate. I spoke about my experiences as a trainer and a human resource consultant, as well as my work with my partner in our family business. I told Ron that I grew up near one of the plants he would be leading and mentioned that my own family placed a high value on hard work and education. My story seemed to soften Ron, and he began to fill me in on his own background and ambitions. He started to talk about what he might want to learn from a business coach. Our work had begun.

In the first few months of our work together, it was critical that I have a good picture of Ron in his day-to-day activities, so I shadowed Ron, observing him in action at all three of the plant locations. To complement my observations, Ron completed numerous tests and leadership assessments, and I interviewed his peers, his management team, and his manager about his effectiveness as a boss. Once I had gathered all this information, I prepared a comprehensive report summarizing the results, and we met for a full day to review the data. The goal was for Ron to identify any gaps between what his intentions were and what others perceived. And there were significant gaps.

Ron thought having a tough exterior would be seen as motivating, and he thought evoking fear would drive others to high performance. So, he was surprised and defensive when it became obvious from the feedback that Ron's tough and intimidating exterior only made others keep bad news from him, avoid revealing their errors, and cover up their mistakes. Once he had time to reflect on the feedback, Ron understood that his leadership approach was flawed. Only then did he begin to ask questions and resist a natural temptation to blame others. He made a concerted effort to address those behaviors, which we both agreed might derail his rise to the top.

He worked hard to change from "just a numbers guy" to a leader. Ron was not an easy boss, and he would never be particularly easy. But he was fair and willing to change, and he wanted to help advance and develop others. These traits were obvious, and he became a role model to others on how to manage feedback and use it to make personal changes, even when the feedback was difficult and painful to hear.

Ron wanted to broaden his understanding of leadership, so we found articles, books, and journals to help him understand the research on leadership and, specifically, what made a corporate leader successful. He began to read business journals and books, taking the lessons appropriate to his role and putting them into practice. He then began the hard work of building his team and taking on difficult projects, marking the beginning of his steady climb to the top of this historic company. Within ten years, he was an executive vice president and chief operating officer. Ron ultimately became known for his ability to create safe environments and develop strong leaders.

I consulted with and coached in Ron's company for more than three years. As he continued to advance in his role, we worked together to build his team and create a culture of learning in collaboration with the company's human resource professionals. I am sure that one of the reasons Ron and I were compatible was because of our shared values: loyalty, family, responsibility, integrity, and education. We built trust through these values and that foundation allowed us to discuss difficult topics.

One of the first difficult topics we discussed was the bat in the corner of his office. Apparently, when he was agitated, Ron would pick up the bat and tap it on his desk to signal his displeasure. It was wildly inappropriate, of course, and naturally his managers did not like it. In one of our coaching sessions, I asked him, "*What's the deal with the bat, Ron?*" He replied, "*Oh, it's funny; people are obsessed with it.*" I then said, "*Well, it doesn't work for a top leader to even suggest violence, so if your goal is to be seen as a top executive, you'll get rid of it.*" In our next meeting, it was gone. We never mentioned it again. Ron told me years later that he kept the feedback report I wrote at the beginning of our work together. He said that he would read it from time to time to ensure that he would never become complacent in his role.

KEY QUESTIONS

I often reflect on this assignment, the lessons I learned from Ron and his team, and how we built such a trusting partnership. Here are some of the key questions I've asked myself:

- Was my working-class background a factor as Ron and I engaged with his management team? I remember feeling a little vulnerable when I revealed my educational background and my late entry into the professional world.

- Did my transparency play a role in creating a bond between us?

- Most importantly, what did I learn from the experience, and how would I ensure I continue to do what worked so well?

Leadership Lessons

Ron continued to be successful in his career in the years after we worked together. I took the lessons I learned from him to my work with other executives throughout the next twenty years. It turns out the hard hats, the steel boots, and the people I encountered were well worth the trip to that office with the bat parked in the corner. Here are six leadership lessons I took away from the experience.

Don't overlook the middle

This early assignment was one of the most interesting and rewarding of my career. I thoroughly enjoyed learning how the product was made while walking the plant floor in boots and a hard hat. I was also exposed to the importance and competence of the middle manager. Those who are in the middle are often a forgotten group and receive little attention from management, academics, and business schools. Yet, the middle manager is often the person who deals with the day-to-day issues that affect the lives of many employees, especially in a manufacturing plant. Many of Ron's employees had grown up in families with generations of experience in the industry. The work was dirty, hot, and uncomfortable, but the middle managers had the equivalent of a PhD when it came to their area of the plant.

Focus on developing others

Much of what I learned from Ron and from this assignment was about the diverse aspects of a leader. Ron was demanding and often abrupt in his interpersonal style, yet he was successful within his company and with his team. Ron's model of leadership was a unique reflection of his values and ambitions. I often asked myself what he had that resonated with his employees. The plant floor was his domain, but the corner office was his ambition.

What was it that gave him the ability to lead and live in both worlds? I believe now that it was Ron's focus on developing others. This desire to grow leaders and teach them how to deliver results was anomalous in Ron's industry. His approach to development was not driven by the human resource manager but by himself. He knew almost everyone on the plant floor, he knew the business, and whenever possible, he gave his employees a chance to learn. He often asked them to take on something challenging, different, and exciting. This was his superpower. He was a leader who wanted others to learn, and his employees knew it.

Define your own authenticity

"Authentic leadership" is a popular term in management theory and is currently being studied by organizational scholars, with a plethora of definitions on hand. While being authentic may be a laudable goal, what it means to be authentic is better defined by you. It is the individual with a unique set of values, goals, and behaviors that fit a personal style. And Ron's personality was authentic and fit perfectly within the culture of his industry. His style was direct, honest, and consistent. He was not warm and fuzzy, but he was also not cruel or too blunt with someone who was failing on the job. When someone was failing, he would give them direct feedback on their performance. I never heard him make his feedback personal— it was about the job, not the person.

The term "authentic" can mean being open and honest about your feelings and reactions, even if you need to manage those feelings sometimes. But being direct and honest can be overdone and can be perceived as selfish, arrogant, and driven by ego. Authenticity does not mean expressing everything you think, either. It is not sharing all your frustrations and problems, telling your team about your difficult relationships, or talking about your irritations with your boss. It is not sharing corporate gossip or engaging in backroom political spying. And yes, there are leaders who rationalize all these behaviors as authenticity, but I wonder whom this openness is serving.

Authentic leaders serve the organization and the employees. Authentic leaders know themselves and are open to meaningful conversations with supportive but challenging mentors, partners, and friends. They stay in touch with their values. Authentic leaders understand the concept of power and how power must be managed. They are the type of leaders who connect, even with a poor performer, with kindness and empathy. This type of authenticity is motivating and inspiring. Ron knew what he valued, he knew he was ambitious, and he challenged himself. He was not easy or, relaxed or warm, but he was described as real and honest. I observed Ron moving and thinking too fast for small talk, and he could appear rude when stressed. Yet, when faced with a safety issue in the plant or when he was unintentionally harsh with someone on his team, I could see him quietly and with no unnecessary drama, address the issue, change his behavior, and apologize when necessary. Is this authentic? I think so.

My hope is that you will define for yourself what authenticity means to you and how it appears in your behavior with others. I encourage you to stay close to that definition and pay attention when there is a gap between the leader you intend to be and the leader others see.

Revisit your values

As a leader, it's important to revisit your values every year. Performance review time is the best time to remember, reevaluate, and restore your values. Take a good look at your top five values and ask yourself some tough questions:

- What really matters to me?

- How am I living these values?

- Have my priorities changed?

- Is it time to reevaluate? For example, could ambition take a lower priority as I face retirement? Or does my value for adventure become less of a priority once I have my first child?

There should be time each year to restore trust in your values with a thoughtful reflection on how your values shape decisions. Think about a time when being certain about your values helped you change. Was there a value that motivated you to take on something new and challenging? Ron had never talked about his values before we met. But once he did, these values became a focus for him. Awareness of his values allowed him to better understand his actions, adapt his behaviors, and inform his decisions. In a situation where he could see that hard work mattered and integrity was critical and where he would learn something new, he was confident that no matter the outcome, he was not crushing his values.

Approach fads with care

The business world is full of buzzwords—like "vulnerability." While encouraging openness and vulnerability is a popular idea within the management consultant domain, I encourage aspiring leaders to approach these attributes with care. Understanding the role of vulnerability within the context of organizational culture is complex and requires more than a TED Talk. Knowing when to embrace openness and vulnerability requires insight. While a well-educated scholar with a movie star smile and a brilliant presentation style can build wealth and status through books and podcast advice, I encourage you to be skeptical. While the experts might have useful and well-researched ideas, it may be impossible to implement these in your day-to-day work.

Top executives—with vast responsibilities to employees and boards—are often looking for a quick fix, the silver bullet, and thus try to demonstrate the newest idea in their leadership approach. "Oh, this vulnerability seems like a good idea," they think as they become attracted to the newest fad. From desperation, they then try to force the ideas through the company with workshops and programs to teach employees something new, but it is a rare program that can meet the expectations of everyone, especially the employee base. The effort then becomes an expensive and time-consuming gap, leaving behind a confused and cynical workforce.

When faced with new and innovative ideas like vulnerability, thinking fast or slow, or other innovative concepts, make sure you do your homework. Take the time to investigate, collect data from your team and your workforce, and design experiments to see how the new ideas will help the company meet its goals. You know your company better than any consultant, management professor, or coach, and so does your top team. Once you have sufficient support and input, you will find the implementation of these new ideas becomes easier and is more likely to succeed.

Ron was open to the latest innovations. He attracted management experts who were interested in reviving a legacy industry, and these experts became part of Ron's efforts to educate his workforce. The messages of these experts were often entertaining but made no difference in the perspectives his employees held about the company. For example, Tom Peters (whose bestselling book, *In Search of Excellence*, is still considered by some as a classic recipe for corporate success) was a powerful speaker, and Ron's bosses and employees cheered wildly for him. Yet, all of Peter's advice had little impact on Ron's efforts to make substantive changes in how the company did business.

Another entertaining speaker was Jerry Harvey. Jerry created something called the Abilene Paradox, which was an interesting story that, in theory, would warn corporate decision-makers from making flawed decisions. Decisions are often risky and difficult so Harvey's story, while entertaining, did little for the individual manager sitting at his desk figuring out how to manage that budget. The ideas behind the Abilene Paradox were useful yet, the decisions made by Ron and his company's leadership continued to be flawed and almost destroyed the company. Look inward first to your knowledge of the company culture, norms, and the unique circumstances you face. Then go to the outside experts, and your own team to decide, make change and search for innovative solutions.

Have fun

I do not think there was any day in the plant when Ron was not having fun. He loved the energy, the work, the people, and the product. In my work shadowing Ron on the plant floor and watching him interact with the management team, he was usually very direct, prepared, and thoughtful. He was more like a professional ballplayer coaching the high school team. It was fun for him to show his managers respect and acknowledge their skills, and they loved it, too. He had fun, and that attitude was contagious.

Executives and managers often talk about how they are not having any fun in their jobs and how they want to make a change. In the aftermath of the pandemic, this is understandable. Good for you if you are in a start-up with a basketball court in the game room. For most people, however, fun at work doesn't mean free food and games. Fun means the ability to lead creative assignments, to work with a team of peers who challenge your thinking, and to know you might be making a difference for your customers. Fun is not the false fun of the forced holiday cocktail party—it's the fun of accomplishment. I was once at a baseball game when a child in my row caught a fly ball. The entire team turned and cheered that child, and they were losing the game! Fun is available. Find it for yourself and help your team find it, too.

References

Field, E., Hancock, B., & Schaninger, B. (2023, July 17). Middle managers are the heart of your company. McKinsey Quarterly. https://www.mckinsey.com/capabilities/people-and-organizational-performance/our-insights/middle-managers-are-the-heart-of-your-company

Harvey, J. B. (1988). The Abilene paradox: The management of agreement. https://web.mit.edu/curhan/www/docs/Articles/15341_Readings/Group_Dynamics/Harvey_Abilene_Paradox.pdf

Milkman, K. L., & Duckworth, A. (2021). How to change: The science of getting from where you are to where you want to be. Vermilion.

Peters, T., & Waterman, R. H. (2015). In search of excellence: Lessons from America's best-run companies. Profile Books.

Rokeach, M. (1977). The nature of human values. Free Press.

4

THE CAREER COMEBACK

USED TO REFER to my friend Karen as "Karen the Creative." She was the only woman I have ever met with her own wood shop. She was energetic and a brilliant seamstress. She was witty and kind. I met her when we were young mothers in our thirties. She had graduated from a fashion program at a local university and bemoaned the fact that she was unable to attend the Fashion Institute in New York despite having a scholarship. She came from a small town, and her parents were afraid of the Big Apple. After college, she did well anyway, working in the retail industry. Shortly thereafter, she married her college sweetheart and moved to a suburb near me.

Karen never faltered as a creative person throughout her life. She used every moment of her time productively when she wasn't parenting her four children or assisting her husband in his career ambitions. She had numerous forays into creative entrepreneurial ventures. I loved her and was awed by her talent.

When Karen and I met, I was working part-time as an educational trainer, and I was just beginning to understand the limitations I would face without a college degree. Karen and I had different skills and ambitions, but we both recognized that we were not cut out for the life of a stereotypical suburban housewife. Based on this shared outsider perspective, we forged a deep friendship that lasted for decades. I learned many things from Karen, but the lesson that had the greatest impact on me happened when she gave up her creative dreams and began to look for a "real" job.

Karen targeted roles in which she thought she could excel, but what she found when she interviewed for jobs was subtle discrimination, patronizing recruiters, and quizzical looks that suggested she had wasted her talents with her family and business ventures. Karen felt dismissed and discouraged; this job search process had crushed her. She eventually returned to the alumni office at her college and found an administrative job for little money but with the hope of a tuition benefit for her children. Unfortunately, she found the job boring and the boss demeaning. I will never forget one of our last conversations shortly after she started that job and before an aggressive cancer took her life. Karen felt discouraged and saddened by the work, and she had lost the joy of her creative spirit.

A few years later, I had a chance to experiment with a way to help women like Karen return to a rewarding career. I was working as an adjunct professor at a top business school, and it seemed just the right time to see what I could do for women like my friend. I thought I might be able to find a way to use the resources of the wonderful business school where I worked to connect with women who wanted to get back in the corporate game, and I found smart women and men to help me.

First, I enlisted two MBA students, who were also parents, to work with me on a survey. I wanted to find out about the experiences of women with an MBA who were attempting to return to work. They had not just left the corporate world for lack of childcare. They left for many other reasons, which made it very difficult to regain their confidence and their positions in the corporate world. After a year of study—and enlisting the help of a corporate partner, faculty, and administrative staff at the school—we launched the Career Comeback program.

In 2007, we welcomed a group of women to the first cohort, and the program was a success. While some women found jobs, there were others who discovered they were not ready to head back to the corporate world and needed more time to garner the necessary resources and support. We also found women who needed to further their education and still others who needed to restore their self-confidence. All the women in this program found among their classmates a supportive group of peers who served as a network, and they were exposed to other trusted advisers and coaches to help them as they headed into the next stage of their careers.

A benefit of this program was the participants' exposure to world-class faculty and current business topics. The participants realized that their time away from work did not diminish their intelligence and perhaps even enhanced their skill set. Unfortunately, this program was not continued due to lack of funding. But a few small companies continue to work with women attempting to head back to work after a hiatus. One exceptional program is designed and led by a woman who attended that first course at our business school. Since there will always be a need for women to reinvigorate their ambitions, the abundance of programs for these women today makes it evident that my dear friend "Karen the Creative" is still making a difference.

KEY QUESTIONS

Here are some of the key questions that arose as a result of this experience:

- Why do women lose confidence when they leave a job to raise their children?

- Are the demands on professional women causing them to lose their way?

- Given the proliferation of these programs, and especially given the frequency of women who opted out of corporate jobs during the pandemic, has nothing changed? Is it still a difficult slog?

- What would I advise a woman in her early career if she wanted to ensure she could stay on track?

Leadership Lessons

The struggles faced by my friend and the subsequent creation of the Career Comeback program had a profound impact on me. Here are four leadership lessons I took away from the experience.

Confidence is key

Work gives us identity, and therefore, someone who leaves their professional role and takes on a parenting role would find their identity enhanced—at least, that is what I expected. But our study found that women, even those who left work for health concerns or to care for their aging parents, struggled with their identity. In short, the role of caretaker had diminished their confidence. Some of the women felt they had lost themselves. Some women expressed fear that the mundane caretaking tasks had dulled their ambition. Others would explain that they could not fathom how they would be able to succeed in the working world without losing out on their personal lives. Without self-confidence and some amount of personal ambition, it would be difficult to convince an interviewer to take a chance on you. The fundamental task, then, for the participants in any return-to-work program must be confidence rebuilding. Pep talks, inspiring quotes, and motivational TED Talks are ubiquitous. Like cookies, they taste good, but the good taste doesn't last long. It takes more.

I have never seen any study that indicates taking a break from paid work is correlated with lowered creativity, intelligence, or skills. So, no, you do not lose IQ points during a career break. Perhaps you could have done more to keep your skills up to date—there are numerous ways to stay current and sharp. Online course work is one option, and some of these courses can lead to a degree or certification. Staying in touch with industry peers, as well as making sure you continue to read both about your industry and, more broadly, about the state of the business world, is another option. Don't just glance over those articles about leaders who have been successful in managing work and life integration. Pepsi's former CEO, Indra Nooyi, comes to mind. Engaging in these stimulating learning activities will have a twofold benefit: building abilities and rebuilding your positive self-image.

Prepare, prepare, prepare

In real estate parlance, it is "location, location, location" that matters most. In career counseling, the axiom is "prepare, prepare, prepare." Preparation is paramount once you are considering your return to your career after a break. Social media is a great way to maintain your network and let others know you are ready for work. But assuming your new or updated LinkedIn profile will draw people to you is a wrong assumption. You'll need patience and persistence in preparing for your reentry.

Once you have successfully navigated interview websites, practice interviewing again and again with someone you trust. My suggestion is to use the following format:

1 Write down five to ten difficult interview questions—the ones you hope they don't ask.

2 The next step would be to record yourself reading the questions and answering them, then listen to the recording. Do you sound confident? Did you make sense? What did you miss? What would the interviewer hear?

3 Then try this same process again with someone you trust asking you the same questions on Zoom or FaceTime and record the session. Watching yourself, listening to your "ums" and other awkward fillers, is hard and can be ego-deflating, so I suggest that you do your critical reviewing alone.

4 After all of that, you might be ready for a real interview. Once you have done one, always stop and pause before you prepare for the next interview. An after-action review will allow you to assess your feelings about the interview, your interviewing style, what questions stumped you, and what you did well.

5 Now practice again. Come up with ten new difficult questions. While it is doubtful that anyone will ask you these exact questions, you will be more confident, relaxed in your responses, and feel strong when you leave an interview if you practice, practice, and practice again.

Stay in touch

Social media can help with maintaining networks, but you should make it a priority to stay in touch personally. One way to do this is to keep a list of twenty connections who would take your call on a busy day. This list may change over the span of your career, so it requires your attention and cultivation. You may need these contacts someday to give a reference or help you network for a new role. Even if you don't think you will need their help, these are the people who will suggest meaningful projects, connect you to volunteer organizations, or help you find a board role.

The top twenty are people who know and trust you; you have established credibility with them. So, call, write, email, and make sure they remember that you value your relationship with them. Nurturing these relationships means more than a thumbs-up on a text, a hello on Facebook, or a comment on LinkedIn. It means connecting, listening, and having an occasional coffee, lunch, or taking a walk. Recently, *The New York Times* suggested the eight-minute phone call as a way to stay in touch. The idea is gleaned from research that suggests the eight-minute call not only lifts your spirits but also provides the potential for a longer conversation at some later point. Most of us think we will get to that longer conversation some time, but we rarely do, so connect! You should already know who is on your top twenty list, so stop reading now and give one of them a call.

Keep time

Musicians use a metronome for timing. The setting can produce a click or tone, and the beat schedule is set by the musician. This timing helps the musician keep the proper pace while playing. You set the timing for your career based on your financial, social, personal, and psychological needs. Today, we hear terms like the "Great Resignation" or the "quiet quit" to capture our career reboot after the pandemic. COVID brought us to our new home office. Our children often fended for themselves as we struggled to keep our jobs and deliver on our promises. Our older friends and family members faced illness and sometimes death—alone, without us. The pandemic shed a harsh light on our lives, and we reconsidered the pace of our careers.

Each stage and age of life has its own inherent challenges. Honoring those challenges when they arise is the key to a rewarding life. The early years, when your job serves as a classroom where you practice new skills, may be the time when your energy and ambition run unhindered by financial and personal demands. Midlife, when resource demands are unyielding, might be a time when your career takes a back seat to your family or to a more pragmatic attitude toward your financial obligations. When these demands lessen, you may find new energy and pace and decide to advance professionally by switching careers or by accepting a more meaningful role. Some find this is the time to step up to a more complex leadership position.

The idea that your career should be advancing at the same pace for your entire working life can become a trap from which you may never escape. You have numerous roles in your life: son/daughter, brother/sister, husband/wife, parent, friend, teacher, mentor, helper, and so on. They all matter, but they will all change, and some will pass forever. Examine your roles and consider how you feel, think, and spend your time in each role. An exercise that might help you decide which roles you want to nurture in your current phase of life is to write each role on a small piece of paper, then review each one carefully before you "discard" that role by placing it in an envelope marked "Discarded." After you complete this exercise, open the envelope again and review each slip of paper, taking out the roles you want to keep (for now). Decide how each role will impact your time, energy, and self-esteem. This exercise will provide some insight as you consider how you will honor your timing and plan for your future. Whatever stage or age, you are the one who sets the metronome and no matter how difficult, the only tempo that matters is your own.

As your personal and professional priorities change over a lifetime, you may find that stepping away from everyday demands is necessary, and you may feel fear or freedom initially. However, keep an eye on your future, and use your time away to revisit your dreams and plan for the day you step back into your career.

References

Career comeback archives. (n.d.). Wharton Magazine. https://magazine.wharton.upenn.edu/tag/career-comeback/

Dunn, J. (2023, January 3). Day 2: The secret power of the 8-minute phone call. The New York Times. https://www.nytimes.com/2023/01/02/well/phone-call-happiness-challenge.html

Johnson & Johnson supports the "Women Back to Business" program at the University of St. Gallen for another two years. (2021, September 16). Johnson & Johnson. https://www.jnj.ch/social-commitment/women-back-to-business

Mcleod, S. (2023, August 2). Erik Erikson's stages of psychosocial development. Simply Psychology. https://www.simplypsychology.org/Erik-Erikson.html

NSCC. (2020). Theories of adult psychosocial development. Lifespan Development by Lumen Learning. https://pressbooks.nscc.ca/lumenlife/chapter/theories-of-adult-psychosocial-development/

O'Neil, D. A., & Bilimoria, D. (2005, May 1). Women's career development phases: Idealism, endurance, and reinvention. Career Development International. https://www.emerald.com/insight/content/doi/10.1108/1362043051059830/full/html

Rothbard, N. P. (2001). Enriching or depleting? The dynamics of engagement in work and family roles. Sage Journals. https://journals.sagepub.com/doi/10.2307/3094827

Vasel, K. (2021, June 1). These return-to-work programs could help moms reenter the workforce. CNN. https://www.cnn.com/2021/06/01/success/returnship-programs/index.html

Women Back to Work: DEI and Returnship Experts. https://www.womenbacktowork.org/

5

THE SERVANT LEADER

S TEPHEN WAS THE newly appointed CEO of one of the largest coffee companies in North America. The company, in its heyday, commanded over sixty per cent of the coffee market with more than 5,000 locations. A budding entrepreneur could purchase a franchise and build their kingdom. Stephen's appointment to CEO was akin to becoming royalty. Stephen was ready to take the helm, but this iconic company was going through some changes, and he knew he had significant challenges ahead. In an effort to enhance his leadership skills, he attended an executive program for CEOs. When he heard a former CEO speak about the importance of having an executive coach, Stephen found his way to me.

During our introductory phone interview, I was impressed with Stephen's thoughtful questions about my experience and coaching approach. I could hear his passion and optimism about the company and its future. He had a calm, understated manner matched with practical insights about the company and his leadership team. When he asked if I would travel to meet him and his team the following week, I was happy to say yes.

Stephen had been a member of the company's top team long before his appointment to the CEO role. He did not aggressively seek the role of CEO, but he was a trusted and well-respected executive so when the board began to explore new leadership, he was a prime candidate. The board and Stephen were aware that certain issues had been long avoided or ignored as the company grew. Environmental concerns, lack of workforce diversity, increasing competition, and complex tax liabilities were affecting the brand reputation. As a result, years of goodwill from the public began to unravel.

Stephen had been preceded in his role as CEO by a beloved leader and major shareholder. The board saw Stephen as a steady hand to guide a peripatetic leadership team, and they hoped he would realign the corporate strategy. One roadblock Stephen would face as he attempted to bring the company forward was an onerous people problem. The former CEO, who was now chairperson of the board, had mentored an ambitious young vice president named Daniel with the expectation that he would be catapulted into a C-suite position. But this expectation and Daniel's frustration would prove to be one of Stephen's biggest people problems. Almost everyone felt that

Daniel wasn't ready for advancement to the C-suite, and they hoped that he would learn the complexities of leadership under Stephen's calm guidance. Daniel had a strong focus on sales, he was charismatic and bright, and he was extremely politically savvy. However, he had not demonstrated strength as a visionary and strategic thinker.

After a few months as CEO, Stephen felt pressure from the board chair to appoint Daniel to a major leadership role. Tensions began to grow because Stephen knew Daniel wasn't ready. Subsequently, Daniel began to aggressively undermine the substantive change agenda driven by Stephen. Soon, it became obvious that Stephen would need to rely on his strong values and his leadership philosophy, both of which would be tested in the next few years.

Stephen's values were centered on responsibility, integrity, loyalty, family, and faith. Stephen was clear on his philosophy of leadership, and he referred to himself as an advocate of servant leadership—a concept defined in 1979 by Robert Greenleaf, a former AT&T executive. Greenleaf wrote in his first essay that the servant leader should serve others first and operate as a steward of the organization as a whole. In the 1970s and 1980s, this focus would transform the more autocratic style that dominated the field of leadership. But as the decades advanced, it would not account for the disruptive changes in corporate cultures that began to take precedence. The digital revolution, increased business consolidation, advancing a global company focus, workforce restructuring, shareholder advocacy, and the shameful rise of executive pay would come to dominate business decisions as we advanced toward the new millennium. As a result, the idea of serving the employee *first* took a back seat to a more aggressive corporate style.

When Stephen, who had good intentions to serve his company, gave the coveted role of COO to a competent and well-liked executive, Daniel was angry and hurt. He created conflict and drama, distracting the top team with emotional outbursts and backroom political maneuvering. Stephen would spend his first six months as CEO pacifying the board chair and calming the culture. As we worked together, he was diligent in his efforts to adapt to this reality and press on with change efforts.

Stephen was my client for almost two years, and we built a trusting and respectful partnership. While in some of his efforts he was unable to adequately address the intractable political backstabbing, he did stall the ill-advised advancement of the board chair's favored executive. He was also able to build a climate of continuous learning and excellence that survives today.

KEY QUESTIONS

I often wondered if my positive impression of Stephen from the very beginning caused me to be blind to the realities of the dysfunctional culture of his company. Here are some of the questions I have since asked myself:

- Is it possible that Stephen's humble and kind approach was a problem? Perhaps he should have had a more aggressive approach as he dealt with the politics of the board.

- What else could Stephen have done to be more supportive of Daniel and to allow him to flourish?

- Should Daniel have had more feedback from a strong human resources executive?

- How could we have involved the board in our efforts to address the distractions that thwarted Stephen's attempts to place the right people in the right positions?

- Did I ignore what I knew about a company culture and the undercurrents that distracted change efforts?

Leadership Lessons

Stephen's values never failed him. It was an honor to learn from him what servant leadership really means. Here are six leadership lessons I took away from the experience of coaching Stephen.

Choose a coach carefully

The coaching profession has become a commodity. That is both good news and bad news. The good news is that coaching, which was once only available to executives at the very top of Fortune 500 companies, is today available to most everyone within a company. In the past, though, this resource was delivered by well-trained psychologists and organizational experts with advanced education in human development and organizational dynamics. This is part of the bad news: today, anyone, regardless of training or education, can and will hang their shingle as a coach. There is currently no agreed-upon educational or qualifying criteria for coaching, although the work of the International Coaching Federation has been a leader in defining excellent standards.

What does this mean for you if you are looking for support and help in your career? I suggest you consider the Latin expression "*caveat emptor*," which means "let the buyer beware." Many experienced coaches have found themselves cleaning up an organizational or leadership mess made by an inexperienced and unqualified coach. When choosing a coach, keep in mind that you need someone who can help you diagnose your weaknesses and your obstacles to success. You need someone who will ask a lot of questions, even those that are awkward and uncomfortable. It is difficult to really learn much if you are never uncomfortable. Remember, you need an open mind to learn.

Stephen and I spent almost an hour together on our first phone call, and he asked great questions. He also listened carefully to my responses. He was very interested in how I would approach the work of coaching, what my attitude was toward keeping information he shared in confidence, and, especially, how we would measure results. I suggest that you follow Stephen's methodology:

1. Ask someone you trust to offer a referral for a coach. Try to find the most qualified person you or your company can afford. Select someone who has both the education and the personal fit you'll need to be successful. Resist the temptation to be starstruck by a fancy degree, charisma, or charm. The coach must know how organizations and people learn, grow, and change. It can be beneficial if they have former business experience, but if it was from decades ago, be sure they have continued to stay informed on current business concepts and theories. I don't know about you, but my career health is as important as my physical health, and I would never hire a medical doctor just because she worked in a hospital twenty years ago.

2. Interview the coach by asking questions that help to reveal their background and training in the field of coaching, as well as their approach to coaching, their experiences, and how they will measure success. You might ask questions like:

- What is your approach?

- What might I expect from you?

- How will you maintain confidentiality?

- What is your role in following up on our conversations?

- How do you measure results?

- What obstacles should I anticipate in terms of our engagement?

- How will you know we are focused on developing the right skills for me?

- What goals should we have, and how will we know if these goals are the same goals my boss has for me?

3 Be thorough, and leave no stone unturned. Stephen expected me to meet with him face-to-face for a final interview, and I was willing to do this without compensation. Today, this is easier because we can trust Zoom interviews. Stephen also expected me to complete a full round of interviews to help him focus on the areas he needed to learn more about or improve in as he took on the CEO role.

If you follow Stephen's approach to choosing a coach, you will weed out the impostors and ensure the relationship is a good fit for you.

Mind the gap

There is often a gap between the leader you think you are or want to be and how others experience your leadership. In Stephen's case, he was committed to being a servant leader, and his desire to serve was often in conflict with the aggressive, dismissive behavior of a few executives reporting to him. Yet, his persistence and his patient, steady hand became his superpower in light of the changes his company was going through. He never wavered from his values or his servant attitude, although he often adjusted his perspective and continued to work to make certain there would be no gap between his intentions and his observable behavior.

I fondly remember a story that indicates the kind of leader Stephen was and why I found him to be admirable in his leadership role. On his last holiday as CEO, and because he had company employees serving in a war zone, Stephen agreed to join military leaders who were heading overseas to greet the troops. Despite the obvious risks, he went. He talked with the troops and served them a meal. He confided in me that he was frightened and anxious when they came under fire. He thought about the fact that he only had to experience this for one day, but the troops must feel this way every day. When I asked him if he had told others about the trip, he said that he didn't want to publicize it and that it wasn't his style to talk about it. But the troops on the ground were certainly aware of his presence and his support—and that's what mattered.

Dilute the drama

When in the throes of a meaningful change, and as defined in *Leadership on the Line: Staying Alive Through the Dangers of Leading* by Marty Linsky and Ronald Heifetz, leaders who are making significant mind-set-related changes can be pilloried. They become the first ones out the door once they challenge the status quo, often because they are seen to bear full responsibility for driving change. They are perceived as forcing change and often encounter resistance to anything new. In reality, an organizational change often requires new thinking, and that type of change must come from the top but also from those who are in the trenches. Yet employees in a change effort often find they are uncertain about their ability to adapt to new realities, and they will need to learn new skills, shift their priorities, and experiment with new behaviors and a new mindset if they are to survive a reinvigorated corporate reality.

Yes, it is important to honor the successes of the past, but it's the future successes that will matter. The drama of change is evident in disruptions like the one experienced by the taxi companies when Uber brought them to their knees or when Zillow's website usurped the local real estate brokers. Employees resisted change because of uncertainty and loss because anticipated successes for the future were not assured. However, reducing the drama and distractions for employees is critical, and it takes a focused CEO to understand how to minimize the fear of change and increase the excitement of future possibilities. The culture of this company was steeped in the past and exploring the underlying realities of the norms "under the surface" might have provided data that we could use to drive change.

Take "me" time

Sometimes, a top leader will have to deal with backroom decisions that no one knew about, secretive offsite meetings, and a steady stream of difficult and tense meetings. All of this will evoke feelings of isolation and exhaustion. This can cause burnout and poor decision-making, and it's important for a leader at any level to find a haven for renewal. Time with family, friends, and trusted advisers will provide the top team members with an opportunity to restore their energy and reestablish their professional mission. While Stephen was able to evoke a calm presence, his dedication to mentoring young people and his dedication to his family both served as a resting place to restore him within the turmoil of a changing organization.

Stay the course

There are always tradeoffs when you lead. Stephen realized he would lose some of his most loyal colleagues, friends, and peers because of his role in implementing changes within the company. When he was maligned and criticized, he felt hurt and disappointed, but he held on to his values and his vision for the future. His investment throughout his career in building strong relationships and his constant integrity and competence benefited him. Despite his rocky tenure at the top and his eventual, abrupt departure from his CEO role, he found his loyal friends did not abandon him. He went on to establish new business ventures with optimism and confidence.

Face failure

As a society, we have such a conflicted relationship with the word "failure." Anyone who has ever attended a leadership program has been inundated with inspiring quotes about the role of failure. One of my favorites, which has been attributed to Albert Einstein, is: "*A person who never made a mistake never tried anything new.*" In business, failure can cost too much. You could lose your job, hurt your employees through flawed ideas and strategies, damage your reputation, and damage the company. But, failures at the very top are often ignored or minimized after the CEO leaves the company. There are many recent examples of CEOs who have become front-page news after leaving their companies in disarray. Failing at any level in an organization is often a fatal blow to your career. There is, though, one certainty about failure—it is a meaningful learning experience.

I can almost see you rolling your eyes. However, try this exercise, and you might be convinced that failure could be your learning partner. With paper and pencil, draw a line from your first job (that ice cream server or babysitting job is more important than you may think, so don't eliminate those early work experiences) to your next job, and a line from that job to your next job, and so on. Then, note all the moments of success and failure. Also, note the skills you used or the skills you needed but did not have. I think you might find that you learned from both successes and failures, but because of human nature, failures seem to teach the best lessons.

What happened to Stephen? He went on to experiment with new entrepreneurial ventures, and he now has a happy life. He is collaborating with people he knew and cared about in his former role as CEO and has mentored and advised young people on their career journeys. I learned so much from him, and I saw first-hand how hard change could be. I saw that what looks like failure can enrich a career and teach lessons never learned in a classroom.

References

Brown, B. (2010). The power of vulnerability. Brené Brown: The power of vulnerability | TED Talk. https://www.ted. com/talks/brene_brown_the_power_of_vulnerability? language=en

Seppälä, E. (2014, December 11). What bosses gain by being vulnerable. Harvard Business Review. https://hbr. org/2014/12/what-bosses-gain-by-being-vulnerable

Sime, C. (2019, March 27). Could a little vulnerability be the key to better leadership? Forbes. https://www. forbes.com/sites/carleysime/2019/03/27/could-a-little-vulnerability-be-the-key-to-better-leadership/ ?sh=cf47f8c783e8

What is servant leadership? (n.d.). Greenleaf Center for
    Servant Leadership. https://www.greenleaf.org/
    what-is-servant-leadership/

Zapata, C. P., & Hayes-Jones, L. C. (2019). The conse-
    quences of humility for leaders: A double-edged
    sword. Organizational Behavior and Human Decision
    Processes, 152, 47–63. https://doi.org/10.1016/j.obhdp.
    2019.01.006

6

GLOBAL GIFTS

O N A BEAUTIFUL spring morning, over coffee, I met with Rebecca, who was leading the non-profit efforts of the executive education programming for our school. She mentioned that she was preparing a proposal for a Wall Street investment firm, and she was having difficulty motivating our faculty to lead the program. She wondered if an adjunct professor, which was my role, might be interested. Rebecca knew me, and she thought my interests would be a good fit for the course leadership, especially since I was known as an advocate for women's leadership, and all the participants in this new program would be female business owners.

"*Why don't the faculty members see this as something meaningful?*" I asked. Rebecca took a breath and said, "*Well, probably because the courses will be taught in the Middle East.*" She smiled sheepishly and added, "*It will be a difficult commute.*" I replied, "*Well, I'm still interested despite the commute.*" And the adventure began as I traveled to this university for the next five months in my role as faculty director. This program, funded by an investment bank, was designed to address the needs of female entrepreneurs. Initially, it was focused on women in emerging economies. The dean of our school was convinced that we could launch the program with meaningful course work and continue to advance our reputation and women-oriented initiatives.

Our team consisted of administrators, small business experts, adjunct faculty members, a recent MBA graduate with a training background, and selected external and internal faculty members. Our staff and faculty traveled to the university every month, and we created course content appropriate for an audience of female small business owners whom themselves traveled from countries in the Middle East. The topics were designed to enhance the business acumen of the women in the program: marketing, strategy, leadership, and teamwork, as well as skills in networking, negotiation, communication, and more.

The generous funders of this program hoped the women would gain the knowledge they needed to scale their business ventures and learn how to create a business plan that would attract funding. But as we began the program, it became evident that the complexities of working with two educational systems, as well as the differences we encountered in culture, teaching approach, language, educational background, and attitudes about gender, would require a singular focus—building a team of collaborators to ensure a successful outcome.

The participants' admission to the first iteration of the program was based on the revenue their businesses had generated, their educational achievements, and their stated goals for growing their respective business enterprises. The applicants included travel agents, real estate developers, bakers, private school owners, jewelers, and non-profit community leaders. The program was delivered at a Middle Eastern university, where the participants were expected to board throughout the four weeks of the course. This residency requirement was difficult for women in this conservative Muslim culture. Despite many obstacles, we finally had over twenty women who were ready to learn.

On our first morning in a Cairo classroom, we met interesting, kind, excited, open, and smart women who were more than willing to work together and build group cohesion. We knew that the group's ability to work together would be essential to the success of this endeavor, and these women immediately knew how to connect with one another. However, connecting and engaging with faculty members was more difficult for this first cohort. That connection was important because most of our faculty members would expect a lively debate in the classroom. Robust interaction relies on dialogue, questions, and challenging ideas and concepts, especially in a business school. Yet, in many cultures, professors have historically been distant and unavailable to students, and students are reluctant to ask questions or express disagreement with a professor. Eventually, this hesitation diminished in our classroom though, and as the weeks passed, the confidence and competence of the student entrepreneurs grew.

These women were determined to gain skills, knowledge, and a network that would launch their small businesses into the next level of growth. It was a pure joy to work with them, and they inspired me and our team. This first cohort brought forth inspirational leaders who learned what they needed despite the language barriers, a challenging curriculum, and the stress of being far away from home in unfamiliar circumstances. This first small group ignited what would eventually number over 100,000 women just like them: attentive, committed to learning, strong leaders, and role models for others. These were women who would take their small enterprises and build them beyond everyone's expectations. On the program's closing day, we celebrated by inviting funders, friends, and students to join us, and each woman had a chance to share her strategy, plans, and ambitions for the future.

Looking back, I wonder what it was that really resonated with me when I was asked to lead this initiative. As I worked with this program for six months, I had an exhaustive travel schedule, and the work took precious time away from my family. The Global Gift program continues today. The changes they have made are mostly related to the creation of online course work options and I do wonder if the connections among the participants are as strong as they were when we had our first graduation back in 2008. Of course, political and economic changes have taken place in the region where many members of our initial group worked and lived. Initially, I stayed in touch with our graduates for years after the program, but now I only "see" them on LinkedIn. I still think of them often and hope they have been able to sustain some of the learning and self-confidence they had on that graduation day as they continue to face the future.

KEY QUESTIONS

Looking back, and despite the challenges in this leadership role and my obvious delight in these women, I do wonder what difference we made. I have questions about the value of this endeavor for me, and for them. Questions like:

- Did my value of adventure cost more than I anticipated, and was the timing of this endeavor ideal for my family?

- We never really understood why our faculty members were reluctant to take on the teaching challenge of this program. Should we have done more to engage skeptical members of our world-class faculty?

- Did we ignore the massive cultural differences between our team and our students?

- While we functioned well, we rarely, if ever, stated our overarching purpose and values as a team. Was this a mistake, given the challenging nature of the assignment?

- Could we have done more for the students? Less?

Leadership Lessons

I felt so fortunate to be a part of this program. Over the years, I have watched it grow and change in ways that our team could never have imagined. I learned from each person on my team and from every woman in the first cohort. As I continued my work as an educator, coach, and consultant, I considered the work I did in this program a high point in my career. Here are four leadership lessons I took away from the experience.

Be honest with yourself

You may have opportunities throughout your career when someone asks you to lead an exciting initiative, and you may wonder, "Is it worth it?" I felt ready to say yes as soon as I heard about the program. It was a good fit with my values, and the timing seemed right. This opportunity also resonated with my sense of adventure. But there was a price to pay that I did not anticipate. There was an impact on my personal energy, my commitment to other clients, and my desire to spend time with my young grandchildren. I thought I was ready, but I did not take the time to consider the impact of saying yes. I don't regret my decision, but I'm convinced that if I had been more thoughtful about personal goals, I would have handled my decision differently. Timing matters. So, when an enticing opportunity comes your way, make sure you take the time to reflect on your values, your strengths, *and* your limitations.

It takes some preparation to be ready when asked to take on an exciting leadership role, and your answer will have little to do with your skill set. Preparing to step up to a robust learning experience, one that will take you to the edge of your leadership, with impressive responsibilities and high expectations, will rigorously test your priorities, relationships, and your very self. Self-knowledge, though, is not something you can read about over the weekend while you are considering an assignment. Self-knowledge is acquired over a career lifespan. If you are able to stay open and reflective, you will find that each job, every performance review, the courses you take, the books you read, and the people you surround yourself with will provide you with insight. Then, when you step up to a challenge or back away from one, you will feel confident in your decisions because you will know what is important to you, and you will think about how your decisions will impact your life. Take steps to know who you are and what you care about so that when opportunity knocks, you can answer with confidence and no regrets.

Harness corporate politics

Workplace politics can be tricky to manage in educational institutions, and the Global Gift program was no exception. The team from our school found itself facing a group of faculty members from our host institution—and even some within our own—who were skeptical, cynical, and outright offended by the program. Why? It was perceived that this program was a payoff for Wall Street bankers looking for redemption from the mistakes of 2008. There were comments about the funding ("These people are greedy sharks"), the women-only participants, and the time-consuming travel requirements. Yet, the dean wanted this program to happen, and he knew it would mean an opportunity to influence women in this part of the world. He was someone who could use his vast network to get things done despite the political quagmire driven by the faculty naysayers.

"This place is so political!" I have often heard a client say this about their company culture, using the word "political" as a negative, but is it always negative? Without political influence, how do you gain acceptance of your ideas from those in power? Peter Block, an organizational consultant, offers a simple but powerful template to use when hindered by "politics." Spend time thinking about those people your idea will impact and determine who might trust you and love your ideas. These people are your allies. Also, think about those who don't trust you and never agree with your ideas. These people are your adversaries. Do not forget to consider those who don't trust you but regard the idea as good for them or the company. These people are your bedfellows. Finally, you might want to think about your opponents—those who trust you but still don't trust the idea.

TRUST AND AGREEMENT

HIGH AGREEMENT

Bedfellows   **Allies**

LOW   HIGH
TRUST   TRUST

Adversaries   **Opponents**

LOW AGREEMENT

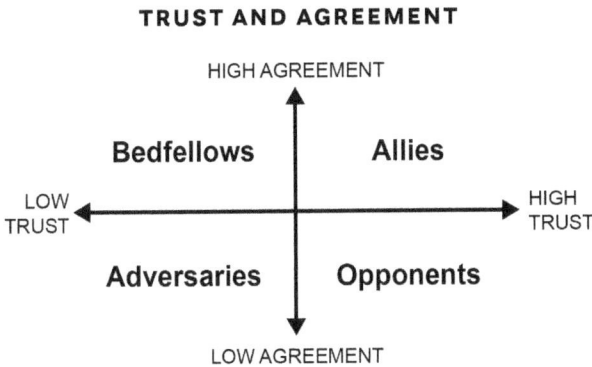

Place the names of each person you need to influence in one of these categories and plan an influencing strategy. You might want to set up a time to talk with each person individually, with the goal of increasing their trust in you or adding more color to the initiative—allowing them to get on board. Now, these actions may be considered "being political", but the naysayers may change their mind after learning more about you and about the impact your initiative has on the company. Who knows? You might find your idea on the company's list of best innovations of the year!

Adjust for the task at hand

On my dragon boat crew, the leader during a race is the drummer. Practices are typically held without a coach on board, and the job of making decisions regarding weather conditions is given to the most experienced paddler. The role of the leader is undefined. A successful team has a clear, shared task, set and established boundaries, and the right membership to achieve the goal.

The Global Gift team adjusted the leader role based on the task at hand. Administrative support members managed logistics and budgeting; their work was paramount as we navigated numerous travel schedules. Faculty and trainers managed the business content. Human resource professionals and I, as the organizational psychologist, managed the group and helped students navigate personal issues. The entire team would meet frequently, and we gathered feedback from the students daily to stay on track and manage any difficulties. With a focus on the purpose and mission of this initiative, we were able to address and handle conflicts with ease since the overarching goal was to support the students and help them build a community with one another. This was despite how varied attitudes to conflict.

However, we could have been more transparent about our goals and spent time together reflecting on the mission we were trying to achieve and acknowledging our disagreements. I think this would have boosted our failing energy during those long days and long commutes and built a stronger bond as a team. Yet, we knew our success was dependent on the students' success. On our last day with this first group, our efforts were rewarded. The students spent most of their time affirming each other and committing to long-term collegial relationships as they headed back to their home countries, their small business efforts, and their families.

Create emotional contagion

Have you ever caught an emotion? It works like this: you are feeling cranky, and your friend hops in the car with a smile, and you are listening to great music as you head to the beach. Your friend is bubbling with joy, and without really understanding why, you are suddenly singing along with her to the Beatles. Or you could be the one bubbling over, and she sinks into the car and immediately shuts off the radio. Without conscious knowledge, your mood shifts. This is known as emotional contagion, whereby you "catch" a mood, like catching a cold or a virus. A masterful teacher, colleague, and mentor, Doctor Sigal Barsade, introduced me to the concept of emotional contagion. It influences a team, a leader, and the culture.

I think our Global Gift team was so focused on the good intentions of the program's goals that this first group of women caught our spirit and energy. The good intentions that we all had for one another were especially evident when we would catch negative emotions (fear, anger, frustration) from others. One of us would make a joke or talk about how wonderfully a student was doing, and this would shift the mood. All of this would happen unconsciously, and suddenly, we would find ourselves having fun, feeling grateful, and smiling at the good work of the participants. What made this work was our respect for one another, an adventuresome attitude, and the goal we shared—empowering women. Even after the recent loss of my dear mentor, Professor Barsade, I still find that catching joy, fun, and love while working to help others catch those emotions from me is an investment in productivity and pleasure.

I took so much from this experience: connections with the women in the classroom seats and those on our team; shared kindness, fun, courage, and openness; and a spirit of adventure. All of this created an exceptional classroom for me, and I have carried my learnings throughout my career.

References

Barsade, S. G., Brief, A. P., & Spataro, S. E. (2003). The affective revolution in organizational behavior: The emergence of a paradigm. In J. Greenberg (Ed.), Organizational behavior: The state of the science (pp. 3–52). Lawrence Erlbaum Associates.

Barsade, S. G. (2002). The ripple effects: Emotional contagion and its influence on group behavior. Administrative Science Quarterly, 47(4). 644–675.

Buddhapriya, S. (2009, January 1). Work-family challenges and their impact on career decisions: A study of Indian women professionals. Sage Journals. https://journals. sagepub.com/doi/10.1177/0256090920090103

Haas, M., & Mortensen, M. (2016). The secrets of great teamwork. Harvard Business Review. https://hbr.org/ 2016/06/the-secrets-of-great-teamwork

Vogt, J. W. (2012). Winning support for your idea. Society of Actuaries. https://www.soa.org/news-and-publications/newsletters/the-independent-consultant/2012/february/ind-2012-iss37/winning-support-for-your-idea/

GOING UP?

OVING ACROSS the country was only the first risk Richard took when he assumed the helm of a food provider that had been established in the nineteenth century. His first few weeks were a rude awakening: a disruptive and deceptive sales rep, a dysfunctional board, and a bloated staff were draining the resources of the company. Everyone's eyes were on him as the savior. Could he fix all this? His human resources partner thought he could, as did the recruiting firm that hired him after a national search, and so did Richard himself. Yet, he was sure he would have a lot to learn. In his previous job, he had a remarkable record as a top sales producer, but he was stalled in his advancement. He wanted a top CEO job—so he answered the call of the recruiter.

Richard was ambitious and ready to make the leap to something that would challenge him, and he also wanted a platform for the next stage of his career. When his human resources partner suggested a coach, he immediately called and asked me to interview for the role. I liked him from the start. He had a calm, Midwest demeanor. He seemed open to learning, and, while self-assured as a skilled sales leader, he understood he had no experience as a CEO. He thought he needed advice and support as he faced what he called "the reality" of this new role.

The new job did not turn out to be the same job the headhunter sold him. In those first few months, Richard unearthed a myriad of problems haunting the company. He wanted to face these head-on, but he was also clear-eyed about the major transition he was going through. He was advancing from a role as an executive who drove sales in his last company to the CEO in this new company. He knew it might be a rocky road, and I was impressed with his commitment to getting insight from an executive coach. We thought about our work together as the start of his advanced leadership learning since a new role can serve as a personalized leadership class. My job was to help him find and use the resources he would need to leverage the learning from this leadership experience. Over time, Richard demonstrated resilience, strong personal and professional values, a kind and empathetic style, and a desire to do the best for the company.

Patricia was another client who was advancing in her career. She was surprised by the challenges she faced when she took her first position as CEO. She had been very successful in her career at a top government agency, and now she was selected to lead a well-known non-profit. She would become the CEO and successor to an icon who had started and led this women-based NGO for decades and was considered a wise elder in the industry. But Patricia, like Richard, found the reality of the business was far from the ideal described by the headhunter and board members who recruited her for this role. Her situation was further complicated by the star power of the retiring CEO—a powerful force, internationally known, well respected, and greatly admired. Patricia felt akin to a small-town choir director being asked to take on the role played by Lady Gaga in the movie *A Star Is Born*.

Patricia faced a tough audience. When she had time to assess her situation, she found fairly complacent staff, entitled board members, and a skeptical donor base. While all this was fixable, given her skills, she thought a coach would be a helpful support as she navigated the first year of her contract. She wanted someone with business savvy who could fortify her leadership with resources and insight. But she also wanted someone who would operate with compassion and kindness as she shared her vulnerabilities. A colleague of mine knew I was particularly interested in working with women in new leadership roles, and so happily, Patricia and I started to focus on her introduction to the new role. Over the next few years, when the assignment was completed, we became friends. I watched over the years as her creativity and innovative spirit achieved results well beyond those of the former CEO. She continues to lead this organization, updating not only her organization but the industry, and she has been building a global reputation as a thought leader in her field. She is the icon now.

Richard and Patricia possessed commonalities: ambition, intelligence, and a drive toward excellence. Both were risk-takers, as well as being thoughtful *and* decisive leaders. They demonstrated the courage to make tough personnel choices and had the empathy to understand the impact of those choices. Both Patricia and Richard shared an enthusiastic commitment to the mission of their enterprises and to their employees. For Patricia, this mission had worldwide implications, and for Richard, the mission was to preserve the excellence of this historic company and to create a pathway for long-term success as he mentored and inspired the employees.

As we worked together, both Richard and Patricia were clear on their goals and were enthusiastic about the values they would bring to their jobs. This focus was the ballast that would hold them each steady as they faced personal changes, economic downturns, distrustful employees, and a pandemic. Today, happily, they are both actively running their businesses, and I consider them role models for the modern CEO.

Patricia and Richard also faced similar issues as they stabilized their businesses over the years: a change in structure, firing long-term staff members, rebuilding their leadership teams, addressing global demands, experimenting with new lines of business, and adjusting to economic instability. But they both, at least initially, had to deal with a major distraction and disruption to their efforts: a difficult board.

In Richard's case, board members would openly challenge his decisions and attempt to undermine his confidence. In contrast, Patricia's board had become complacent; they were living in the past and were not the advocates and supporters they had been in the earlier years of the organization. The stress of dealing with boards often caused these two competent leaders to question their decisions, and it became evident early on that the culture of the board was as important as the culture of the company. Managing board relationships was taking much of their time and energy, and neither Richard nor Patricia had anticipated the impact of these board dynamics.

As first-time CEOs, they had both made assumptions about the role of the board and the relationship between the board and the CEO. They came to their roles with confidence that board members would be their natural collaborators and act as trusted advisers on important company decisions. Yet, the board members often operated as adversaries. Boards can establish habitual norms based on personalities, capabilities, and power dynamics. Even with a new CEO, it is very difficult to change the climate of a board with long-term members.

Richard had to deal with a powerful chair who, in the past, had been able to use his position to coerce employees, threaten other board members, and shut down discussions of issues he personally did not agree with. With Richard on board, he continued to operate this way, and there were times when he very publicly attempted to impose his will on Richard. Patricia also had to deal with board members with long tenure. Some of them had become more focused on their warm relationships with one another than on the strategy and advancement of the organization. For both Patricia and Richard, these boards were, in their unique way, a burden. They wanted to change these dynamics, although they took different paths to change the board relationships as they advanced toward new goals.

Patricia relied on the help of the board network and the most knowledgeable members to address the complacency and move some board members to an "emeritus" status. She was then able to refresh the board with innovators who focused on growth and had the capabilities to advance that growth strategy. Richard had more difficulty. He tried to accommodate the disagreeable chair and build a relationship with him. He also tried to compromise and use the other board members, with less power but more competence, to influence the chair. He even went outside the board to find past leaders to advise him. Ultimately, he focused on his vision for the company as a priority and took a new tack. While he was respectful, he started to take actions he thought best for the company despite a conflicting view from the chair. He met aggressive challenges with a firm stand, and while not always successful, he continued to advance his goals for the company.

In my work with these first-time CEOs, I learned how important it was to help a client manage their anger and frustration about the organizational culture they inherited so they could move forward in their role and learn from the job they had, not the job they thought they would have. Often, their desire to prove themselves worthy of a CEO role caused them to take action too soon since the notion of defining your success within the first ninety days was embedded in their thinking. The first ninety days, as these two learned, were best used not in frustration but in learning about the business, listening to their employees, and trusting their own insight and competence. It takes longer than ninety days to set your team in motion. Of course, there are issues that need to be addressed, even in those early months, but often, a too-aggressive stance and making immediate structural changes backfires. It is difficult for a new leader to take the required time to collect information and data. But the data will be immensely beneficial, and thoughtful strategic change can follow.

Since both Patricia and Richard also felt they needed to revamp their business strategy and develop their top team members, they also needed to manage their frustrations with their respective boards and resist the temptation to take the disagreements personally. Eventually, it was their steady hand and considerable business acumen that helped them rebalance their approach to the job of CEO. Both leaders have been successful in their roles despite the extremely challenging business environment of the pandemic years. Today, board members face more scrutiny and accountability, so Patricia and Richard's investment of time in building strong boards of capable collaborators has brought success despite the rocky start. While these two newly minted CEOs were industry experts, they could have been vulnerable to short tenures if they had become too distracted by their boards and board personality conflicts.

KEY QUESTIONS

Here are just some of the questions I pondered after coaching these two exceptional leaders, both of whom continue to "go up."

- Should I have anticipated the difficulties these CEOS would face with their respective boards before I agreed to coach them?

- What happens when there is a blurring of roles and conflict between board members and senior team members?

- Should I have taken the time to interview board members before each assignment and, therefore, been more equipped to anticipate issues?

- When taking on a top job, how might a candidate assess a board?

- What is the impact of disappointment, anger, and resentment a new CEO might feel once it is clear there has been a bait and switch?

Leadership Lessons

Here are four key leadership lessons I took away from the experiences of coaching Richard and Patricia.

Analyze assumptions and modify expectations

Making assumptions can derail even the most committed and competent executive. I encourage my clients to consider the framework offered as "the Ladder of Assumptions," as designed by management experts, as a tool to use when onboarding a CEO, especially when that CEO is you!

Ladder of Assumptions

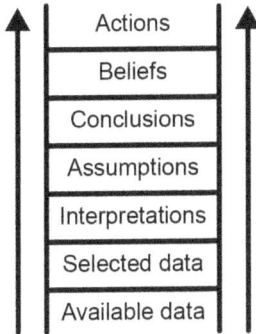

Actions
Beliefs
Conclusions
Assumptions
Interpretations
Selected data
Available data

Of course, we rarely take the time to evaluate our assumptions. This seems especially true once you are on the exciting ride of a major life accomplishment. The importance of considering how your actions will be influenced by your background and beliefs cannot be minimized. Your beliefs filter, often unconsciously, how you draw conclusions about appropriate actions—and often, those beliefs drive you in the wrong direction.

Learning to analyze your assumptions will allow you to modify your expectations and notice the influence of an overly positive or negative reaction to what you observe. While I did not use this tool directly with Patricia and Richard, in our earliest conversations, we did discuss their disappointment and shock regarding the state of things when they took their respective CEO roles. Had they been more aware of their assumptions long before they arrived at their first board meetings, they might have been able to adjust to the realities of board dynamics and planned their influencing strategy well in advance of any board conflicts.

Observing a board in action before the final contract is signed would be ideal, but that's improbable. Instead, why not interview a few key board members with your antenna tuned to how they perceive their role? Could you observe how power is dispersed among the board members? Once you have some data based on your observations, you might use the Senge and Argyris template (see this case reference: https://

www.toolshero.com/decision-making/ladder-of-inference/) and ask yourself some critical questions to check your assumptions before you create a plan for rebuilding your board.

Pay attention to power dynamics

Every corporate or not-for-profit has some version of a board of directors. This is the executive committee serving in a joint supervisory role for the organization. However, the duties of a board are unique to each industry, and the rules and regulations are often defined by the board members or the industry. Today, the responsibilities of a board vary, given the forced accountability of board members because of the pandemic. Today's board members find themselves developing remote work policies, making decisions about vaccine mandates, and reaching beyond their former advisory role to stabilize the shaky and stressful atmosphere of their companies.

Boards in 2020 found the norms they had formerly established (size, frequency of meetings, and formal and informal rules defined by government regulations, corporate laws, and the organization's mission) needed to be shifted. As the pandemic wanes, it will take time for a board to reestablish and define its culture. But make no mistake: it is the culture of the board that determines their commitment to shareholders and employees. The board and CEO relationship can be contentious or collaborative, but as Unilever chairman Michael Treschow has suggested, "*It's important to create confidence with the CEO that the board is his/her best friend and supporter, helping him or her to develop the business.*"

We all have those moments where we struggle to deliver on what seems to us an impossible request. In this situation, you will attempt to use your source of power and influence to get things done, access what you need, and meet the goal. You use what power you must to influence others. Power, according to a pivotal study done by social psychologists John French and Bertram Raven in 1959, can be based on your status as the legitimate boss, based on your relationships with others, or even simply on your knowledge and expertise.

Bases of Power
As described by John French and Bertram Raven

Positional Power	Personal Power
Legitimate Power *(e.g., the boss)*	**Referent Power** *(e.g., admiration, respect, affiliation)*
Reward Power *(e.g., a bribe)*	**Expert Power** *(e.g., special abilities)*
Coercive Power *(e.g., a protection racket)*	**Information Power** *(e.g., what you know)*
Resource Power *(e.g., access control)*	**Connection Power** *(e.g., who you know)*

Once we think we have a source of power, we like to try it out. Just this week, I observed how even an eleven-year-old understands the use of power. On a rare visit with my grandson, he used the power of my relationship with him (called "referent power" in academic journals) to influence me to change my mind about sugary cereal. So, I found myself having a breakfast not of champions but of sugar. Another example came later the same week when a computer expert influenced me to purchase a high-priced modem … I don't know if I needed more power (no pun intended), but I thought, "Well, she is the expert, and she probably knows best!"

Power is not something you think about when you take on a top job, at least not explicitly. Our newly launched CEOs, Richard and Patricia, knew they would have the power to hire and fire their leadership team, but they had not explored or considered the legitimate power of the board. Richard was faced with the chairman's ability to dilute the CEO's message by using his long-term relationships among board members to challenge Richard's efforts. Patricia, on the other hand, had not considered how the power of the close board relationships had distracted her board from their fiscal responsibility and focused their attention elsewhere.

Power conversations can be awkward, but just a cursory view of the topic will arm the rising CEO with a framework to consider as they take on the vast responsibilities required of the role. In the very first months after taking on a position as a top executive, it will help you advance over the arc of your career if you pay attention to power dynamics and use your own power—not to manipulate but to inform, inspire, and motivate. Power will help you build partners on the board as they become aligned with your vison.

Handle conflict with care

Friends, colleagues, former bosses, family members, alumni groups, Google, coaches, consultants, peers, and your former professors are all within your reach. All of these resources could provide information, support, and ideas when you are faced with a conflict. This is especially important when you are on unfamiliar turf in a new company. So, why don't we approach others to hear their perspectives?

In Richard's case, he was reluctant, at first, to go beyond his easily accessed mentors and me, his coach, to explore how he might manage his recalcitrant board chair—possibly because he did not want to be seen as ill-prepared for his first CEO role. However, once he was more confident and had spent time digging into each aspect of the business, he moved from avoiding conflict to a more competitive and confronting style. Richard was not naturally inclined to confront or compete, but he began to realize he needed to change his conflict style if he was to strengthen his relationship with the board. He was right, too! His last few years have been much less contentious, and he learned valuable lessons when he shifted his approach.

A simple matrix developed by Kenneth Thomas and Ralph Kilmann posits that conflict requires either an assertive or a cooperative attitude, and we tend to default to one habitual style, even when it's not effective. Changing in the midst of an important new role takes courage, but making a change might be your only chance to achieve those lofty corporate goals.

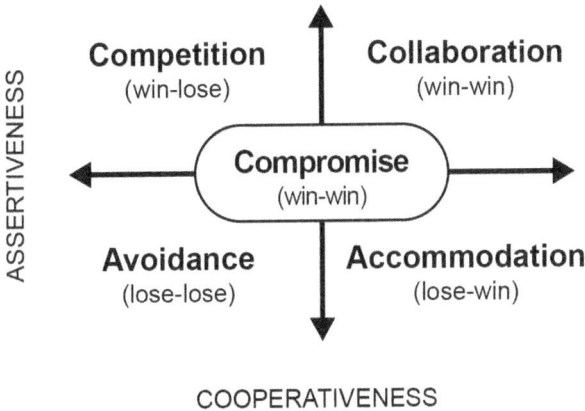

ASSERTIVENESS

Competition
(win-lose)

Collaboration
(win-win)

Compromise
(win-win)

Avoidance
(lose-lose)

Accommodation
(lose-win)

COOPERATIVENESS

Patricia was initially inclined to confront the more complacent members of her board and felt annoyed and disappointed they had never addressed the financial challenges facing the organization. Patricia even considered forcing some of the kind (but unfocused) and committed board members to leave their positions on the board. But she also knew she had to change her style. While she avoided confrontation with the full board, she took time to work with a few influential members and create a plan to compromise on how they all might be able to reset the board's priorities. In addition, Patricia collaborated with a professional network of female CEOs, and she learned important lessons from more experienced executives on how to manage complex board relationships.

Manage your emotional state

Advancing in your career, without exception, will bring both joy and disappointment. When I encounter a client who has achieved the recognition and advancement they have long desired, there is a palpable energy and excitement in those first few months and, surprisingly, a sense of loss and disappointment as well. Making a change and moving to the top always means a loss of long-term colleagues and company relationships. Both Richard and Patricia made a geographical move that required family members to adjust to a new home-base. They lost their former peers and colleagues and now encountered direct reports who responded to their new CEO with a reserved approach. Sometimes, their new leadership team members were too cautious and often too obsequious. This type of experience helps explain how a CEO becomes isolated and protected from bad news.

I experienced this when I returned to work the day after I defended my dissertation, and I was now "Doctor" Monica McGrath. While I was excited about my new status, others would remind me that I was "not a real doctor." I also encountered a former boss who was clearly irritated when someone asked me about my new degree. "*Okay, okay,*" he said. "*Now, let's get back to work.*" While I thought I was discreet about the new PhD, I was also surprised and disappointed at these microaggressions. I had assumed others would be supportive and pleased, but the corporate culture during this time was overly competitive, and my disappointment turned quickly into frustration. It was only a few months later that I began to look for another job.

Managing these negative and positive feelings falls in the realm of emotional intelligence. You might be thinking, "Oh, no. Not EI again!" But yes. Your ability to use and manage your emotional intelligence requires you to access your self-awareness and manage your emotional state. This is an essential ability for any leader. When you make major changes in your role, pay attention to your moods and understand what and who might trigger your emotional state. Once you become aware of how your emotions are operating, write about them. Writing about your emotions and why you are triggered and sharing thoughts about your mood with a trusted adviser, coach, or friend who listens without judging will help you contemplate your actions. This will help you refrain from angry outbursts and overcome inaction when you need action. This will also allow you to use your emotions to drive the energy needed to achieve your vision.

We are all unique combinations of our health, background, education, and experience. Even the most resilient and competent CEO is, in fact, human and her emotions are often on display. Knowledge and awareness of these emotions will provide data to drive behavior, and it's not just the CEO who needs to know themselves—we all need this. Today, Richard and Patricia are still active and committed CEOs, and I'm extremely proud to have played a part in their journeys. They were two exceptional people open to learning and willing to change their approach when they needed to do so. Now, as they teach and develop their successors, they bring knowledge, compassion, and wisdom from past experiences that will have an impact far into the next decade.

References

CEOs eye 2022 with optimism and a dash of uncertainty (press release). (2022, January 24). Deloitte United States. https://www2.deloitte.com/us/en/pages/about-deloitte/articles/press-releases/ceos-eye-2022-with-optimism-and-a-dash-of-uncertainty.html

Cox, J. (2022, January 12). Inflation rises 7% over the past year, highest since 1982. CNBC. https://www.cnbc.com/2022/01/12/cpi-december-2021-.html

French and Raven's five forms of power. (n.d.). MindTools. https://www.mindtools.com/pages/article/newLDR_56.htm

Johnson, C. (2017, June 5). Council post: Three essentials for a successful CEO and board chair relationship. Forbes. https://www.forbes.com/sites/forbesnonprofit

council/2017/06/05/three-essentials-for-a-successful-
ceo-and-board-chair-relationship/?msclkid=dfb9317f-
d13011eca45d1f2db9bb777B&sh=46ac251b5ba5

Mulder, P. (2018). Ladder of inference model explained.
Toolshero. https://www.toolshero.com/decision-
making/ladder-of-inference/

Victor, D. A., & Turner, M. C. (n.d.). Leadership styles
and bases of power. Reference for Business. https://
www.referenceforbusiness.com/management/
Int-Loc/Leadership-Styles-and-Bases-of-Power.
html#ixzz7WNYJucWn

Watkins, M. D. (2013). The first 90 days, updated and
expanded: Proven strategies for getting up to speed
faster and smarter. Harvard Business Review Press.

8

THE NEW BOSS

A S I APPROACHED the possibility of retirement,
I had one more goal I hoped to accomplish—to
take on a failing business and turn things around.
I wanted a role with full responsibility for the people, the product, and the financial results. In 2013, I
was offered a role as the vice dean of the university's
executive education division. The job seemed like
a natural fit for me since I had served in numerous
part-time and interim roles throughout the fifteen
years I had worked for the school. I was considered
a "utility infielder" with a variety of leadership and
administrative skills and was always ready to step in
when needed.

I was a director, faculty member, coach, consultant,
course designer, and group facilitator. People knew
me as a trustworthy colleague, a known commodity. Most of my faculty relationships were collegial,
and I understood just how to navigate the constraints
of the highly bureaucratic school culture to get things

done. So, once I closed out my consulting and coaching practice, I was ready to step into a new challenge. I was full of ideas, enthusiasm, and data from a recent engagement survey of the members of the executive education staff. The survey seemed to indicate an organizational climate in trouble. Low morale, confused communication, and a palpable distrust and anger with faculty and administrators were evident. My idea was to reset the culture with a focus on the excellence of our faculty and restore the educational mission of this division.

And as for my enthusiasm? After my first month and more than fifty interviews with staff and faculty, my enthusiasm had waned. Employees felt victimized, naive about the competitive landscape, and angry yet complacent. I remember thinking, "I did say I wanted a challenge!" I got to work. With a group of faculty advisers and the blessing of the dean, we started making useful changes that could bring this fading business back to life. Within the first six months, we seemed to be making great progress as we advanced talented employees, built more transparency with staff, and created higher standards for faculty who delivered program content. Things seemed to be steaming along splendidly, but there was a change on the horizon, and soon, our efforts would come to a halt.

The dean who hired and trusted me was ready to return to teaching. Within a few months, we had a new dean, and I had a new boss. When I met this charming but inexperienced former professor, I was suspicious. It seemed that he was not interested in the long-term changes we needed but came aboard to use his role as a stepping stone to his next big job. He took time to remind others, often, that he was the "smartest guy in the room." Watching him dismiss and embarrass lower-level employees was painful.

When it became evident that he was making a backroom effort to remove me and undermine our change effort, I knew our plan to renew the business was in trouble. Eventually, he reengaged with some of his more obsequious friends, and they began to dismantle the organization, drive divisiveness within the culture, and marginalize me. There were many years when this division of the university could claim a stellar reputation for delivering valuable educational insights to thousands of students, but once this self-promoting leader moved on to his next playing field, falling revenue and diminished quality continued to take their toll. By 2020, the pandemic devastated this business, and the loss of prominence continued. Today, with the appointment of a new and qualified dean—with knowledge and experience in organizational behavior—and the advancement of faculty members who are both dedicated scholars and knowledgeable business practitioners, this division is recovering from the past and beginning to show signs of a robust return to success.

KEY QUESTIONS

Leadership and coaching work require self-reflection and the ability to ask honest, specific types of questions in order to ensure you are constantly learning from your experience. Here are some of the questions I have reflected on since this particular experience:

- What was my part in all this?

- What could I have done to ensure that the efforts we had started would continue with a new boss?

- What signals did I miss? And why did I miss them?

- Was there something I could have said or done when I started to lose support and credibility?

- Was I too closed-minded and dependent on the voices of my close colleagues when I heard from those I did not know well?

Leadership Lessons

As you grow in your role as a leader, you will often find that you gain insight from those times when the situation seems bleak. With time, reflection, and personal courage, the career and life lessons that you gain from tough times are often the most profound.

Here are five leadership lessons I took away from this experience.

Take your time

A new boss can be a welcomed change or a disruptive force. A new boss from the inside of the organization comes armed with knowledge and biases that can either help or hinder the efforts of the current staff. A new boss from outside of the organization—from a competitor, a similar industry, or, in my case, a smaller and less prestigious school—can challenge the status quo. It appears that the standard advice from popular management gurus is to "hit the ground running" and make sure those first ninety days demonstrate to everyone your value as the newbie.

But the new boss needs to take the time to learn about the organization and its people and resist the urgency to make a strong first impression. I have seen many newly appointed senior managers face long-term resistance and resentment because they failed to consider the views of their staff. They did not take the time to learn from, listen to, or respect those loyal employees who possessed a thoughtful perspective on the successes and failures of the past.

Remain open

When a new senior executive is brought into a well-established organizational culture, the first few months will often determine the impact and success of that hiring decision. A welcoming attitude is one critical factor in how a new boss is perceived by the team. In this case, I did not exactly put out the welcome mat. My new boss's arrival was met with skepticism by some. He had limited experience. Colleagues and friends spoke openly of his intent to use the platform of the school to advance himself. Many saw him as a job hopper, a manipulator, and an outsider. The hiring of this new dean was a surprise and disappointment to many.

After a frank assessment of my initial reaction, I can see that I was influenced by the opinions of others. I had listened to the skeptics. I was wary from the beginning and found myself unwilling to advocate for the changes we had begun. My annoyance with this new boss caused me to focus less on the goals I had set for the business and more on my job security. I know that I could have been more open, assertive, and empathetic in those first few months.

Question your assumptions

Management scholar Chris Argyris proposed the idea that sometimes we start with a trivial piece of information, and through a series of mental leaps, we often reach an incorrect conclusion. Argyris called this the Ladder of Assumptions, which I mentioned earlier in the book. This occurs when you jump to conclusions without questioning your assumptions and, subsequently, take actions based on faulty or unconfirmed information.

For example, I believed the new boss was only in this job to advance himself, as my colleagues had suggested. When I was ready to advocate for the changes we needed in the business, I based my actions, my frustration, and my disappointments on the premise that he would not be around too long. While my assumptions could have been true, and he might have been as arrogant as I imagined, I based my activities on what I assumed to be true. I never questioned myself, and I never asked my trusted advisers to question me. I was biased. Building a process by which you can honestly check in with others and examine your assumptions is difficult and requires courage. I often recommend that my clients find a small group of advisers to help them keep perspective and resist ego-driven actions.

Seek outside views

Had I sought out advisers, perhaps I would have been asked pointed questions like these:

- What evidence do you have that the new boss is not on your team?

- In what way have you addressed your concerns?

- What would it mean if you were wrong about him?

- What has he heard about the division, and what does he think the division needs?

- Why do you think he will support you?

But I did not hear these questions from anyone, and I did not ask them of myself. If I had, I might have been more confident and direct with him and, importantly, more open to "the new guy." I might have been able to see beyond my ego, and my disappointment. I wonder if this might have allowed me to avoid months of confusion and stress. Would a more objective and informed view have allowed me to push forward our change efforts to revitalize the business?

Rethink your ambitions

In his recently published book *Think Again*, Adam Grant posits the idea that you are better off in your work and personal life if you can rethink your longstanding convictions, opinions, and beliefs. And I agree that rethinking, reframing, and reconsidering sets the stage for a happier and more fulfilling life. But it is quite difficult to rethink your life and work ambitions, especially when you are in the midst of demanding day-to-day decision-making as a leader, yet your ambitions are the lubricant for your actions. While some think ambition is a negative trait, I do not. Ambition drives you toward all those goals that make for a productive and happy life. Over the past few years, during the pandemic, we have seen the ambitions of courageous healthcare workers, teachers, parents, and others drive action and restore our faith in others.

Ambition is a valid and useful characteristic. It is the mature and wise person who demonstrates the self-confidence, resilience, and humility required to rethink personal and professional goals and ambitions in difficult and sometimes impossible circumstances. It is the courageous leader who is able to rethink their goals and dreams when reality has other plans. In this case, I wanted to turn around a failing business. I was sure I could do it, and I was surprised and delighted when I had the chance. Yet, once it was clear that I was being pushed out of the business and the new team was assembled, I resisted reality and took an intractable position. Eventually, I left with my heart heavy and new dreams on my mind.

References

Argyris, C. (1993). Knowledge for action: A guide to overcoming barriers to organizational change. Jossey-Bass.

Boyatzis, R. E., Smith, M., & Oosten, V. E. (2019). Helping people change: Coaching with compassion for lifelong learning and growth. Harvard Business Review Press.

Grant, A. M. (2023). Think again: The power of knowing what you don't know. Penguin Random House.

Schön, D. A. (2017). Reflective practitioner. Taylor & Francis.

Senge, P. (1999). The dance of change: The challenges of sustaining momentum in learning organizations. Nicholas Brealey Publishing.

9

THE TEAM THAT TRANSFORMED

NEVER THOUGHT OF myself as a business school professor, but alas, there I was, standing in front of sixty business school students, teaching leadership and teamwork. It was a little scary and immediately evident that I needed to leverage my corporate career. The professors on this teaching team were at the top of the field of organizational psychology, yet none of them had much corporate experience. So, I thought, if I wanted to succeed in the classroom here, I had better demonstrate my corporate chops. I had a lot of corporate work experience and had coached executives for over ten years, so I did know about the struggles of a real-world corporate executive.

All 800 incoming first-year MBA students at this school had at least five years of work experience, and they studied our business curriculum on campus full-time. Another 150 executive MBA students had over ten years of work experience and attended classes every other weekend while working full-time.

To create a more inclusive and manageable experience for the students, the administration divided the classes into smaller "learning teams" of seven or eight students. This arrangement worked well for everyone. From the perspective of the professor, this meant that students working in teams were able to work together on complex assignments, and peer pressure assured that team members would actually complete the assignment.

These smaller cohorts, which were guided by second-year students, allowed the team members to get to know and understand their peers and to leverage the cultural and business diversity of their team while focusing on a difficult assignment. These small groups were designed to be diverse and often included two or more members speaking and learning English as their second language. Every student carried a very demanding course load, and the first year was intense at this top-rated business school.

All the students seemed to have had enough time in the workplace to understand the importance of organizational culture, yet I felt they would benefit from more than one short course on leadership. Building a management toolkit and enhancing the skills of emotional intelligence, conflict management, and other topics of organizational behavior would add to their repertoire. The management faculty were scholars in their fields of business, but there were too few professors with extensive on-the-ground business experience. I knew that real-time experience leading and following is as important in the workplace as research.

I had an idea that I might experiment with a course based on the learning methodology called "action reflection learning." A course that focused on both real work problems and professional development would add value for the students and would also demonstrate my expertise, experience, and business credibility. Eventually, I found supportive faculty and administrators to clear the path, and the course I envisioned took shape. This course, offered in the last semester of the final year of the executive MBA program, was delivered to a select group of students. I had high expectations that the course would change the perspective of these students and perhaps even be transformative as they reimagined their leadership.

In a former job as an action learning coach and the director of leadership development, I worked with over 100 teams. Our corporate program placed high-potential managers in six- to eight-person teams. The individuals were drawn from every functional area of the business: finance, strategy, operations, human resources, field management, and technology. The objectives were twofold. First, the group was charged with providing a solution to a complex workplace problem to be presented for approval to the CEO. If the CEO agreed the solution was solid, then team members would be accountable for implementation, and their future evaluations would note their success or failure as the solution was executed in the business.

Second, the team members would enhance their leadership capabilities and improve their management skills. This would be part of the presentation to the CEO. Their ability to work on specific skills would be noted on each team member's performance record, and their peers would be observing their progress. Everyone chosen for this program would finalize a professional evaluation completed by their peers and boss and share this with their action learning teammates during and after the program. This would give the group an opportunity to practice new behaviors.

One important aspect of action reflection learning teams is a disciplined approach to personal insight. That is, as one field manager once remarked, thinking about what you are doing or are about to do when faced with a business dilemma. This process of self-reflection helps a manager gain insight on the skills they need to improve as they advance in their careers. Often, this reflective thinking process spurs discovery about how you think and act when working on difficult problems. This type of reflection can reveal behaviors you need to change if you want to effectively lead others.

During the time I coached the corporate teams, I witnessed executives and managers who made significant and profound changes in their leadership behavior because they had time to think through how they behaved in the heat of problem solving. The program I worked with also included feedback and conversations with their team members to add the important views of their peers. Often in our final meetings with the corporate CEO and the top executives, participants would credit the process of reflection as the spark that motivated behavioral changes during the learning team experience. Therefore, when attempting to address the lack of development within the MBA course material, I hoped this corporate program design would provide that same kind of spark for students.

Leadership in Action, as we named the course, was born. Here is how it worked. Each term, we selected six to eight students from a pool of volunteers. The composition of the course over the period we offered it included MDs and PhDs, lawyers, bankers, human resource executives, government officials, actors, military and government leaders, and every level of corporate executive. But the one team I remember as the transformative team—the Team That Transformed—was an exceptional group. They didn't just change as leaders; they became the very definition of transformational leaders. According to the experts, "transformational" leaders not only raise themselves to a higher level of performance but focus on how to ensure they motivate, support, and inspire their followers to this level of excellence as well.

This team was the most open to learning as the course evolved, and they were committed to the premise that leadership learning would take more than one or two advanced courses. They were confident that leadership learning would be a lifelong pursuit. Marian, the group leader, was an inspiring and energetic banking executive who was respected for her ability to organize her time well and for her ability to demonstrate emotional intelligence. She was following her dream as she completed her education, worked full-time, and raised her family. Marian was fully prepared for every class, and she had maturity and kindness that was demonstrated in her attitude. She would go on to apply for and achieve a doctorate in organizational behavior, after she completed the most rigorous MBA programs in the country. Whew! I know that Marian was the linchpin that made this action learning course a learning experience I will never forget.

KEY QUESTIONS

I was curious about the group and their cohesion from our first meeting. I often wondered how, in such a hyper-competitive program, they were bonded together almost immediately. In my reflections during the course and after its completion, I wondered:

- Why did they have such an impact on me?

- What was it in this group that allowed them to build such trust in one another?

- Was there something unique as they evolved that motivated them to be so committed to one another?

- Was there something special in the group dynamics that created their ability to challenge themselves and put aside defensive reactions?

- As their guide, coach, and facilitator, did my interventions and content sessions accelerate their learning?

- Was this group just a reflection and projection of my own trust in and fondness for the members?

- Or could it be that this was just the right course at the right time for the right people?

Leadership Lessons

The joy I experienced while working with this group has stayed with me in every program I have taught since, and my commitment to this model of action learning has also never wavered. Here are five leadership lessons I took away from this truly memorable experience.

Design for action

Action learning is a widely used learning modality that, in simple terms, means any educational program where the learning is done while acting on real work problems. Many executive training programs use a variation of this model. The founder of the methodology is Reginald Revans, who, in the 1980s, described the process by which a group works together with a focus on problem solving and learning. While Revan's design emphasized a rigorous structure for action learning-oriented programs, currently, these programs rarely follow the discipline Revans suggested. Indeed, some educators note that while executive programs are marketed as action learning, they largely consist of practices that don't really get to the heart of what action learning truly is.

In a 2022 article published by *Harvard Business Review,* action learning teams were highlighted as one of the most effective strategies to reimagine diversity efforts. Unfortunately, the expense and time invested by companies and individuals in quasi-action learning programs is wasted when the potential innovation and creativity available from peers are not accessed. These efforts are often given a slipshod design, and the only shared information is polite conversation and stories shared by teammates that highlight a problem—or, even worse, advice about how a team member *should* have managed the problem.

Yes, there is some value to getting advice if that's what you want. However, the value that the action learning approach provides is in the challenging questions, trusting teammates to laser-focus on your problem, and having faith that you will be presented with a new perspective that will help change the way you view the issue. When it works well, action learning respects your view but asks you to put your view aside and consider what you have missed and what you might be unconsciously avoiding. It does this through the insight shared by your peers within the group.

As you move up the ladder of the corporate hierarchy, you often feel pressure to know the right answer. Rarely does a top team member stay open to a new view, even when facing opposition and possible failure. An executive once told me that his employees would run for the hills if he ever said he did not have the right answer to a problem. This fixed mindset attitude can limit your thinking. Action learning teams can help an entrenched manager move from a fixed mindset to a growth mindset.

Psychologist Carol Dweck from Stanford University defines a fixed mindset as closed to learning. This is when the participant believes basic skills, intelligence, and talents are fixed traits, never to be changed. The growth mindset, though, is when an individual believes they could gain competence and skills over time and has an attitude that they can improve their skills, traits, and even intelligence. While we are all a combination of both fixed and growth mindsets, changing a fixed mindset is the key to learning. Of course, all of this must take place with those you trust. What might happen in a safe atmosphere is a willingness to experiment with new behaviors and attitudes. Designing this type of experience can create what happened for the Team That Transformed, and when done well, it can happen for you or your teams.

Know the group

The composition of the group, their personal communication styles, and their experiences all play a vital role in how they will operate and learn. When you assemble working groups and they know they are also expected to focus on learning, it is particularly important to assess their motivations and openness, especially when they are in the heat of problem solving. The linchpins of this Team That Transformed were the leader and the group's desire to leverage their relationships and the work they had done during the MBA program. The leader, Marian, helped design our curriculum. We began the course with a personal assessment for each participant that captured feedback from their school peers, work colleagues, and even faculty. Every group member focused on at least one skill they would improve on as we worked together.

These were students, but they were all business professionals, so they challenged the idea that they were really a team. What constitutes a team, as defined by the late Harvard professor J. Richard Hackman, is when members have a shared task, boundaries clearly stating who is in the group, and the group has decision-making authority—all factors we discussed when designing the course. The students were also concerned about the small size of this group, so we deferred to what the research indicated was the best size for a team that would be focused on both learning and solving work problems. Small, in this case, is better since communication can become complex and bogged down in a larger team, and collaboration can be more difficult. We settled on a small group, despite a good deal of interest from other students, partly because research also showed that as the size of a team increased, team members' satisfaction decreased.

Interviewing team members in advance and assessing their work experiences is beneficial. By asking them to describe their motivations, ambitions, and goals, you will gain insight into their ability to learn and apply that learning to their life and job. It is possible that randomly selecting participants will not provide a trusting atmosphere, which is essential for members as they closely examine their own behaviors. Once you can connect motivations and ambitions to learning, you will find that interactions, solutions, and professional growth will skyrocket.

In my years of working with this model, I failed my group on the one occasion when I did not take the time to consider who they were, what they wanted to learn, and how they might interact. Setting up a team doesn't mean that everyone agrees with one another—not at all. A real team will argue and challenge one another, but they respect one another, too. The Team That Transformed was able to stand and speak confidently on a platform of trust and openness, and it paid off for them in learning.

Give them room
In this class, the group created the content for each session, and each member facilitated one session with a learning partner. This approach helped them experience a safe environment for sharing vulnerabilities,

and, most importantly, it created an atmosphere for each member to experiment with a refreshed approach and the ability to practice new skills. The group was fully engaged with one another and shared the common goal of enhancing their leadership skills. This commitment to one another helped build cohesiveness, deepen relationships, and create opportunities for the team members to experiment with new behaviors. Individuals could show their strengths and address their weaknesses because they knew and trusted one another.

There were exceptional students in the group; often, we used the term "rock star" to identify an exceptional student. One exceptional student from our school eventually worked in the White House in an advisory role to the president. Another student is a gold medal Olympian. These exceptional team members can be a distraction for everyone. While our group's rock star was a start-up CEO, it was obvious that she was admired and respected, and therefore, she did not become a distraction.

I had learned a lot about managing elite team players from NFL coach Dick Vermeil. Coach Vermeil, a Philadelphia icon, had been a winning Super Bowl coach when he came to my class in 2000 to talk to the students. He spoke about leadership and did not even mention the football skills of an aggressive NFL player. He also shared his thoughts about how hard it was to take a group of incredibly talented and exceptional athletes and mold them into a team, but he was not afraid to eliminate one of his rock stars who, outside of the game, consistently brought trouble to the team. Coach shared that he knew his role was to keep the team focused and committed—not to being the best "one" but to being the best team. As a facilitator of the Team That Transformed, I tried to emulate Vermeil's coaching. This, combined with the spirit that the team brought to the work, helped each team member to feel like a rock star. I thought they were, too.

Go for the goal

Each member of this group had an individual goal but given our desire to follow the Hackman model of a real team, we wanted to be sure to have a shared goal. We struggled to define this shared goal until we imagined the future and the most important skills the group members would need for their next jobs after graduation. Skills that came to mind were the ability to influence others without obvious authority and learning to listen—*really* listen—not just to those who agree with you but especially to those who challenge you. We talked about how they might need to examine limiting perceptions and how they might anticipate the reactions of others to their new degree.

Once we finalized our discussion points, we decided that each member of the group would build and share with one another a short-term and long-term action plan for progress. We were explicit about making a commitment to stay in touch with one another and to measure results and share with a learning partner what was achieved, what was not achieved, why certain goals weren't reached, and which goals might have been redefined.

Remember the coach's role

The role of the action learning team coach is unique. While the learning team is focused on solving business challenges and gathering insight for members to use in their jobs, they are also expecting the coach to keep a sharp eye on their group interactions. An experienced action learning coach is a keen observer with the courage to intervene when things are not working and help the group address any behaviors that distract the team from achieving their goal.

The coach is not your friend. The job of the coach is to support each team member's learning. That might mean noticing behaviors that ultimately will become a problem for a rising-star executive. What is needed from the coach is trust as well as a flawless commitment to professional and personal development. The coach must have high ethical standards and be willing to challenge the group and the individual behavior of any member.

It's a high-wire act when the coach intervenes. The coach must be respectful yet very direct. I had a recent encounter that illustrates the importance of the balance a coach must provide. I observed a team member consistently glancing at his phone during a team discussion. So I stopped the team for a moment and said, "*Dean, we made a commitment to focus on the issue at hand. Do you have an emergency? I see you are looking at your phone constantly.*" He was angry about my intervention and, in a patronizing tone, said, "*I'm listening, but I have another important project going on.*" He then slammed down his phone. I sat silently, but I was also angry now.

Then, another team member remarked that the group had decided to turn off all devices and that they all had other projects of importance. He said, "*Don't we want everyone's input? And you, looking at your phone, is a distraction to all of us.*" Another member of the group suggested a break, and this broke the tension. Dean looked relieved. I felt angry and defensive, at least internally, but if I had not managed these emotions, my impact as a coach would have been diluted—not just for Dean but for the entire group. It's tough to manage your emotions, but as a coach, it is key to effectiveness. Eventually, Dean apologized to me for his outburst and I, now calm, responded with respect, a warm smile, and a reminder that the coach's job is to observe and comment.

In contrast, a coach could also be so enamored by the team, the company, or a member of the team that they ignore or minimize difficult behavior, or overly emphasize positive actions by the team or the team members. The group is hoping to learn how their actions may interfere with their effectiveness on the job. If a coach is only cheerleading and affirming, the group will naturally find it difficult, if not impossible, to challenge one another. We know that the kind of love we have for our co-workers—a mix of affection, compassion, and friendliness—creates a positive team and leadership environment. However, the coach must exercise self-management since companionate love can lead to a coach who sees only the good and does not intervene for fear of making the team or the individual uncomfortable.

Leadership in action did transform, not just change, members of that team. This transformation demonstrated each participant's ability to listen to their spirit, to be vulnerable, and to continue to grow and learn throughout their careers. The students still keep in touch, and they have started businesses, entered politics, and become diplomats and educational PhDs.

References

Dick Vermeil: Leadership through the eyes of a football coach. (2000, October 16). Knowledge at Wharton. https://knowledge.wharton.upenn.edu/article/dick-vermeil-leadership-through-the-eyes-of-a-football-coach/

Hackman J. R., & Vidmar N. J. Effects of size and task type on group performance and member reactions. Sociometry. 1970;33 :37–54.

O'Neil, J., & Marsick, V. J. (1994). Becoming critically reflective through action reflection learning TM. New

Directions for Adult and Continuing Education no. 63, 17-29. (EJ 494 200).

Pedler, M. (1980). Book reviews: Action learning: New techniques for action learning. R. W. Revans. Blond & Briggs, 1980 £7.95 319 pp. ISBN 0 85634 101 0. Management Education and Development, 11(3), 219-223. https://doi.org/10.1177/135050768 001100308

Yeager D. S., Johnson R., Spitzer B. J., Trzesniewski K. H., Powers J., & Dweck C. S. The far-reaching effects of believing people can change: implicit theories of personality shape stress, health, and achievement during adolescence. Journal of Personality and Social Psychology. 106(6): 867-884. PMID: 24841093 DOI: 10.1037/a0036335.

10

A QUEEN OF HER
OWN MAKING

DMITTEDLY, I WAS biased when I walked into Sarah's boss's office that first day. I did not like the reputation of this company. This was a top international software company, and while it had excellent financial results, its diversity numbers were abysmal. I had heard that the senior leadership team was particularly reluctant to provide opportunities for women. I was here to meet Sarah, a manager in the financial division of the company and her boss, the chief financial officer. Her boss had mentioned to the company's human resource partner that Sarah was never going to advance beyond her role as a manager. But Sarah wanted more, and her ambition was the motivation for HR to find Sarah a coach.

The hope, at least the hope of the HR manager, was that if Sarah worked with an experienced executive coach, she could change the view of her boss and take her next career step. I was known by the company because of the work I had done with alumnae in the business school where I had been director of leadership. I, too, thought I could work with Sarah and help her figure out what was blocking her career trajectory. Sarah, a CPA, had just completed surveys about her leadership and a one-year performance review. She hoped that this feedback would help her understand what skills she needed to improve on if she were to take on more responsibilities or a higher-level position in the company.

My coaching process begins with a review of a prospective client's performance data. I add more information by interviewing the client's manager. My hope in this interview with Sarah's boss was to gain insight into the person I would be coaching. I also hoped to make certain that everyone involved in this process—the boss, the coaching client, the human resource partner, and myself as the coach—would all be focused on the same goal. This interview with her boss would be especially interesting to me since the data from the surveys indicated that Sarah had always delivered accurate and timely financial reports, and she seemed to be liked by her team. So, what was the problem? Why was she stalled in her career? Frankly, I was curious and a little skeptical when I stepped into her boss's office.

After we talked a little about my experience and coaching approach, I asked him directly why Sarah did not seem to be a candidate for a bigger role and what exactly she needed to change about her performance to advance further in the company. I mentioned that I had reviewed the survey results and was a little confused since I did not see anything that indicated she would not do well in a new role. "*Was there something more?*" I asked. "*Is there something I didn't see in the data?*" For a moment, he was quiet. Then, he rebuffed my diagnosis. "*You might not know this, but often performance evaluations are more positive than they should be for women. And the 360-degree feedback survey—well, no one trusts those results, so that feedback is irrelevant.*"

He had a point. Currently, 360-degree feedback assessments are used to identify areas of learning for a valued manager or executive. These tools are a useful source of data, when used well, for both the employee and the company. But often, a 360-degree assessment is done ineptly, without the needed confidentiality protocols to ensure validity, and the results will be skewed. When this happens, employees enter into an unspoken agreement to say little about real performance issues, and a concerned employee base finds it impossible to get meaningful feedback.

"Okay," I thought. The written performance data is flawed, so let me try to find out more. I suggested that Sarah's boss tell me the real story about Sarah. He began by referencing how she was perceived in senior team meetings and his opinion that she wasn't the right fit for a more senior role. He thought she had no leadership presence. I asked him to help me understand what he meant by "leadership presence." Does she talk in meetings too much? Too little? Does she come unprepared? Now, he was clearly defensive. *"I'm sure you know what I mean,"* he said.

My experience taught me that the term "leadership presence" often means that the person in question just doesn't fit with the culture of the company or the boss's concept of leadership. When someone uses this term, I always ask for a behavioral definition, but rarely are the specifics observable. The implied meaning seems to be: "You don't fit my idea of a leader." The term is a way to disguise bias against someone. While often unconscious, it is unfair and hurtful.

At this point, I strongly suspected that no matter what Sarah did to change her approach, she was probably going nowhere in the company. This coaching effort was meant to distract her from her expressed goal to achieve the next level of responsibility. I needed to learn more and challenge my own assumptions, too. So, I asked for more specifics about her skill set, her team, and her results. These questions also got me nowhere. Her boss admitted Sarah was always well prepared for meetings, and she rarely made errors in the presentation of data. The only negative thing he could say was that he was not comfortable having her in senior leadership meetings. She was a bit too loud, and she often attended these meetings wearing a ring on every finger. Well, I guess these rings were what triggered the coaching call. Now, it was clear this coaching assignment was designed to mediate a gender clash.

I faced a conundrum. Should I take the assignment? If I did, should I tell Sarah my assumptions about the culture of discrimination within the company? Would it be helpful for Sarah to know that her boss was biased? Should I confront the boss about this bias? Should I talk about this with the HR partner? Or should I simply take on the assignment and ask Sarah to remove her rings?

My decision was to design a scaled-down version of the assignment. In our conversations, Sarah reluctantly acknowledged that she, too, thought the company was stalling women's advancement. But she also revealed that her own insecurities often kept her from taking credit for her good work and that she fostered a reluctance to share new ideas. Sarah thought that her working-class background and her state college education made her an anomaly in the company. She felt that she had achieved more than anyone had expected. While she knew she was competent and smart, she questioned her "fit" in the company. At some point during our meetings, I asked her about the rings she wore, and it turned out that each ring was symbolic of someone or something important to her. While the rings were a positive symbol to her, they symbolized to her boss that she was not dressed appropriately and did not appear to fit his perception of a leader.

Sarah wanted some way to manage her anxiety when she attended meetings with senior leaders who might not wish her well. She needed to remind herself to demonstrate an appropriate level of confidence, so we explored ideas and finally settled on a creative solution: Sarah would use an image that reminded her of her worth. We selected the image of a queen, and we decided to use a visual representation she could keep on her desk. While we laughed at that image initially, Sarah promised that during the rest of her time at this company, she would look at the image when she was anxious before a meeting and remember to walk into the room like a queen! She did report to me that she often did this review before meeting with her boss and imagined wearing her cape and crown!

KEY QUESTIONS

Here are some of the questions I have asked myself since this experience:

- What did I learn from Sarah?

- What role did my own negative bias about the company play in my initial conversations with Sarah's boss?

- Was I too hesitant to offer my opinion about the unconscious bias of Sarah's boss?

Leadership Lessons

Here are four leadership lessons I took away from the experience of coaching Sarah.

Temper your reactions to feedback

There is tremendous value in gaining insight from others' feedback. But not all feedback is correct, focused on your skill set, or useful in terms of your personal and professional goals. I remember an exceptionally good boss telling me that he wondered if the feedback he gave me was more about him and what he thought was important than it was about me and what was important to me or to the company. I'm not sure that he was right, but I do agree we often receive flawed feedback from others who do not see us in our role frequently enough or who have a hidden agenda to distract us from a goal.

While it is useful to consider feedback and reflect on its validity, you don't always need to change your behavior in response to feedback. Valid and well-designed tools to gauge your impact on your team and your boss are vital for an ambitious and self-aware executive. But remember to be cautious and thoughtful about taking measures to change your behavior until you are certain the changes are aligned with your goals. If you are asked to participate in a 360-degree assessment, be sure to ask questions about the boundaries of confidentiality, the design protocols, who will have access to the data, and who will help you interpret the feedback. When you understand the data, then reflect on what you need to do next.

A useful tip might be to pay attention to your own emotional reactions to specific feedback. If you find yourself defensive, perhaps there is something you

need to think more about. Or if the feedback is something you have heard before, then it might be a signal
for your attention. Always acknowledge that you have
received the feedback and remember to thank those
who provided it, even if you don't agree with them.
It's important to take feedback seriously, but temper
your reactions with an objective view, if possible, from
others who have your best interest at heart.

Be proactive about nuanced nonsense

While blatant discrimination is easy to spot, it is
often the nuanced bias that confuses even the most
self-aware manager. Corporate tricks can be hard to
spot. However, if you find you are not being invited
to important meetings, don't have access to the data
you need to do your job and find the norm to be confrontation more than collaboration, you should begin
to worry.

Reporting the more nuanced behavior to the
human resource department may lead to your career
demise, and you'll need evidence if you expect the
company to act. When you are uncomfortable and
wonder if you are being discriminated against, or if
you report your concerns and find you are targeted
unfairly, then plan a strategy for the future. A plan
and an outside objective view of the situation you
are experiencing will help you decide your next steps.
Try to pay more attention to your career options to
give you some sense of control and improve your
self-confidence.

No one should tolerate obvious prejudice and discrimination. Never. Report it and leave. But when it's not obvious, you should make sure to keep track of your concerns, talk to former bosses and mentors, reflect on your options, and decide what you can control and what you need to do if your fears turn out to be true.

Know the culture

Knowing what a company values and expects from its employees is essential if you hope to find a role that will position you for the future. It is not easy to uncover a culture when you are searching for a job and even when you are fully engaged in a leadership role. A useful visual often used to define organizational culture is an iceberg. The portion of the iceberg that is visible above the surface represents what the company claims is the way things get done. The portion of the iceberg that is under the surface and not visible to most is how things really get done. For example, on its website, Sarah's company tells me it values collaboration (top of the iceberg). But once you are in the role, you find the only way to be promoted is to compete (under the surface).

To understand the culture of a particular company, ask others who have worked there to tell you what is rewarded, who gets promoted, and why they move up. Read everything you can about the company and use this as data to help you decide whether you want to work there. By using good research techniques,

How companies *claim* things get done

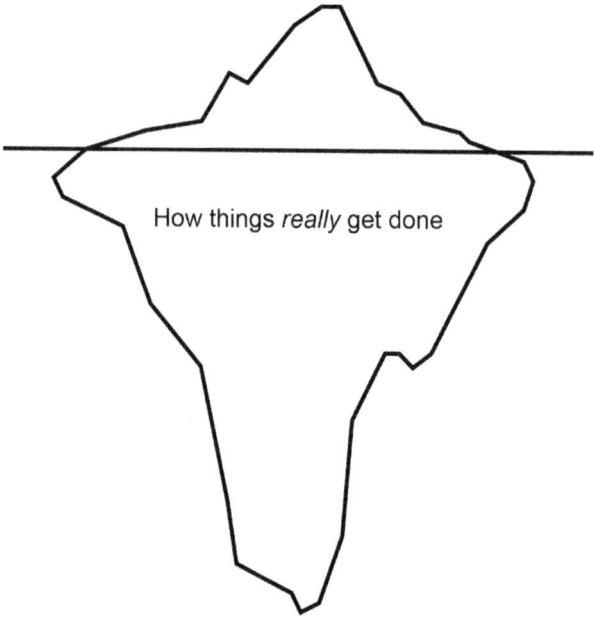

How things *really* get done

you might find just the right place for you to build your career.

Speak up

Women are often hesitant to speak up when they suspect they are facing discrimination. They worry about repercussions. Yet, if you are being sidelined in your job and you have built evidence for your case, the consequences of a biased performance review can change the trajectory of your career. Finding ways to let others know what is happening, and providing evidence for behavior that is questionable, is a reason to speak up. But be sure you are ready when you present your case to those in a position to help. Checking your perceptions with objective outsiders and people who will ask tough questions will prepare you for a challenge.

Yes, there are always difficult people at work. While those who don't like you or don't like what you represent to them are often hurtful, this might be something you simply need to manage. However, a bully, a predator, or actions that demonstrate a blatant bias are not acceptable. You never have to tolerate this. But be prepared when you are ready to take this to the top.

I spoke to Sarah briefly after we finished our work together and after the company began a restructuring effort. She had been offered a financial incentive to leave the company, and she took the offer. When we spoke, she had decided to use this money to start her own financial consulting firm and had recently purchased a boat. Her life was happy; she was wearing her rings, and she was feeling very much like the queen of her life as she was taking a vacation on her boat and finally steering her own career.

References

11 harmful types of unconscious bias and how to interrupt them (blog post). (2020, January 2). Catalyst. https://www.catalyst.org/2020/01/02/interrupt-unconscious-bias

Bates, S. (2003, June 1). Forced ranking. SHRM. https://www.shrm.org/hr-today/news/hr-magazine/pages/0603bates.aspx

Epstein, D. (2016, November 22). Council post: Tips and tactics for a successful 360-degree feedback program. Forbes. https://www.forbes.com/sites/forbeshumanresourcescouncil/2016/11/22/tips-and-tactics-for-a-successful-360-degree-feedback-program/?sh=1c39d5f03fd1

Nisen, M. (2015, August 18). How millennials forced GE to scrap performance reviews. The Atlantic. https://www.theatlantic.com/politics/archive/2015/08/how-millennials-forced-ge-to-scrap-performance-reviews/432585/

Northouse, P. G., & Lee, M. (2022). Leadership case studies in education (pp. 11–16). SAGE Publications, Inc.

Patel, M. (2018, October 30). Council post: Workplace harassment: Why women don't speak up. Forbes. https://www.forbes.com/sites/yec/2018/10/30/workplace-harassment-why-women-dont-speak-up/?sh=1f62446334b3

Ryan, L. (2015, October 21). The horrible truth about 360-degree feedback. Forbes. https://www.forbes.com/sites/lizryan/2015/10/21/the-horrible-truth-about-360-degree-feedback/?sh=6014d6ca69b9

CONCLUSION
WHAT CULTURE WILL
YOU CREATE?

M Y FIRST ENCOUNTER with the importance of organizational psychology and dynamics was in my family's small neighborhood real estate office. Our family had a rule that we all work in the office, and all five of us were expected to become licensed real estate salespeople at age eighteen. I passed the test and found I was pretty good at selling these small row houses, but it turned out I was better at reading people.

My father was the head honcho, writing property advertisements, securing finance, and, surely, he did sell some property too. However, it was my mother who was the heart of the business. She was both a charismatic force and an uber sales demon. She delivered results, but she also set the tone and the culture of the office. In doing so, she somehow taught me how important the invisible dynamics, or those 'under the surface,' really are. That is, how the culture of a business could make a real difference in its results.

Warmth, humor, commitment to one another, and a fierce drive to meet our shared goal of success and nurturing the team—these were the values of our family business. While no one in that small business knew there were business schools teaching future CEOs that an organization reflects their leadership, we knew the climate we worked in was set from the top. That culture provided our family with the means to achieve ambitious dreams.

Leaders who learn

This book tells the stories of leadership—the challenges, the unfair moments, the intrigue behind the scenes, and the warm and nurturing men and women who stepped up to lead. The men and women profiled here worked at every level—from CEO to steel mill manager, from aspiring tech entrepreneur to MBA student team leader. The experiences of these leaders highlight their highs and lows and the actions they took to drive their company culture. The culture they created or the one they tried to change. Every case has a lesson that I learned as their coach. The tips and tools I shared with my clients and the approach I offered as their partner are useful, evidence-based, and easily applied by any leader. But these tools are only one aspect of the leader's success. Those profiled here, and others, many others, had a superpower—a mind open to learning. This—and the ability to trust, to challenge, even to fail sometimes—helped those I worked with drive success not only for their business but for those people who work in their orbit.

Leaders who learn—and coaches who are honored to serve as their coaching partners and sit by their side, also learning, are nurturing a world of dreams and helping others build a meaningful life. I challenge you in your role as a leader. It doesn't matter the size of the organization. The bottom line could be just enough for your small business to get by, or you could be at the helm of a multinational operating in the billions. You could be leading thousands of employees with your approach or just a handful of staff. Regardless, your conversations and your goals matter a lot to those who will follow you. They matter a lot to those who challenge you, too. Take the time to look in the mirror and then open your mind and your heart to learning. I am hopeful that the lessons I learned and shared in this book will become one of your guiding maps. Good luck.

Thank-you notes

As I highlighted in the introduction, I hope this book validates the importance of leadership to my children, grandchildren, nieces, and nephews. I hope my leadership tips might spark new ideas as they manage their career journeys. But, more importantly, I hope this book serves as a thank-you note to all the exceptional people I have met throughout the last thirty years and who inspired me with their courage to lead.

And finally, a heartfelt thanks to you, the reader. You inspire me still. As I begin the next phase of my career and life, I am touched by your courage. I know—you rarely, if ever, use the word "courageous" in your annual performance review, right? However, as I continue to coach in the setting of business school courses and with non-profit leadership teams and the emerging leaders in my life, I am impressed with how often someone raises their hand and takes on a leader's role. Often, their hand is the only one raised. And you, dear reader, might tell me it's just your job, or you want to be seen as a fair leader, or you are not that ambitious and just want to provide for your family, but I don't buy it.

I think if you are open to reading this book, you are open to becoming more. More engaged, more knowledgeable, or more powerful (in the best sense of the word). This, to me, is an act of courage, and I respect and admire your willingness to lead. Thank you for this.

ABOUT THE AUTHOR

ONICA MCGRATH, PHD, is a leadership consultant, business coach, and educator. She formerly served as the Vice Dean for the Aresty Institute of Executive Education at the Wharton School of the University of Pennsylvania. She served in a variety of roles throughout her tenure at Wharton, including Director of Leadership Programs and Adjunct Professor. She also established numerous learning initiatives in her seventeen years at the school. While at Wharton Monica co-created the highly successful Women's Executive Leadership and High Potential Leadership Programs. Monica was instrumental in the design of the Wharton Coaching Network and the Leadership Ventures and Fellows programs.

From 2008 to 2010, she served as the first faculty director for the Goldman Sachs 10,000 Women Program delivered in Cairo and the initial 10,000 Small Business Program, both of which are still in operation. In addition to teaching undergraduate and graduate programs at Wharton, Monica has worked as a consultant and educator within the corporate setting through her consulting firm Resources for Leadership, Inc. Her past clients have included Siemens Medical Systems, Colgate Palmolive Co., FMC Corporation, TDL Group (Tim Horton's), Unisys, Rohm and Haas, DuPont Company, Morgan Stanley, McNeil Pharmaceuticals, Wyeth (currently Pfizer, Inc.), and High Liner Foods. Her non-profit clients have included the Opportunity Finance Network, Women's World Banking, the Kresge Foundation, and the National Philanthropic Trust.

Monica serves in an advisory position for the Wharton McNulty Leadership Program and various executive programs within the Aresty Institute of the Wharton School of the University of Pennsylvania. Her volunteer activities include board leadership with the Philadelphia Outward Bound Board and the Broward College Foundation Board, and she is an active team member on two dragon boat teams. Monica holds a BA in Psychology, a Master of Education in adult learning, and a PhD, with an emphasis on organizational psychology, from Temple University.

www.ingramcontent.com/pod-product-compliance
Lightning Source LLC
Chambersburg PA
CBHW031857200326
41597CB00012B/443